Battlegroun
BOURLON

CW00383127

With the continued expansion of the Battleground series a **Battleground Series Club** has been formed to benefit the reader. The purpose of the Club is to keep members informed of new titles and to offer many other reader-benefits. Membership is free and by registering an interest you can help us predict print runs and thus assist us in maintaining the quality and prices at their present levels.

Please call the office 01226 734555, or send your name and address along with a request for more information to:
Battleground Series Club Pen & Sword Books Ltd,
47 Church Street, Barnsley, South Yorkshire S70 2AS

Battleground Europe

BOURLON WOOD

Jack Horsfall & Nigel Cave
with the assistance of Philippe Gorczynski

Series editor
Nigel Cave

LEO COOPER

First published in 2002 by
LEO COOPER
an imprint of
Pen Sword Books Limited
47 Church Street, Barnsley, South Yorkshire S70 2AS

ISBN 0 85052 8186

A CIP catalogue of this book is available
from the British Library

Printed by Redwood Books Limited
Trowbridge, Wiltshire

*For up-to-date information on other titles produced under the Leo Cooper imprint,
please telephone or write to:*
Pen & Sword Books Ltd, FREEPOST, 47 Church Street
Barnsley, South Yorkshire S70 2AS
Telephone 01226 734222

CONTENTS

Introduction by Series Editor

In 1970, when still at school, I visited Bourlon Wood for the first time. What makes the wood stick out in my memory is that it was there that I found more relics of the war than anywhere else before or since on the Western Front. The reason for this was quite simple - tree felling operations were in full swing, and where trees had come up, roots and all, was to be found a wealth of items such as German leather equipment.

Now I have a rather clearer idea of what makes Bourlon Wood so important. This should be quite obvious to any driver approaching from the western side of it. From some seven miles away, for example (and the weather allowing), on the Bapaume road the dark mass of Bourlon Wood becomes visible, dominating the ground on all sides. It is defended on the western side by the Canal du Nord, then a huge dry ditch, as construction was not completed before the outbreak of war. The wood acted as a last safeguard to the approaches to Cambrai. It is easy to see why both sides considered it such an important objective.

The result of the Battle of Cambrai can best be described as a rather expensive draw. However, it reinforced the lesson that the Germans had taken from the ferocious fighting during Third Ypres: that fixed lines of defence, no matter how complex and how magnificent, were no longer proof against a determined enemy equipped with a sufficient weight of artillery. The tank was a useful addition to the battlefield, but

The town of Cambrai in 1918. The Germans left mines and started fires as they retreated. The photograph shows the town still being shelled as the Canadians enter the main square.

it was severely hampered by mechanical limitations as well as the problem of working over difficult ground.

The Cambrai battlefield (like its near neighbour, the Le Cateau battlefield) is a much less visited battlefield than the Somme; and yet it offers the same good walking, the same excellent views, and memorials and cemeteries of similar beauty and poignancy.

This is the second in the trilogy in this series which concentrates on the Battle of Cambrai. Like many of the *Battleground Europe* series, it does not aspire to bring any new research to the fore or present further arguments in the controversy about the conduct of the battle. Jack Horsfall has taken some of the printed sources and combined the information from them into a battle narrative and accompanied this with an excellent and comprehensive tour of the area - the primary aim of all of these books.

In preparing the tours and material for *Bourlon Wood* both of us have been assisted tremendously by people in the local community, notably the Mayor of Bourlon and his wife. Members of the Flesquières Tank Association have been particularly free with their time and information. Above all we both owe a great debt of gratitude to Philippe Gorczynski, co-author of *Following the Tanks*, who hosted both of us at various times at his hotel, the Beatus, in Cambrai, and gave freely of his time and his knowledge. Indeed, so great was his assistance that both of us had no hesitation in adding his name to the title page of this book.

Nigel Cave
Porta Latina, Rome

Introduction

In August 1914 elements of the German First Army, commanded by *Generaloberst* Alexander von Kluck, stormed through Belgium. Amongst other obstacles he faced a heroic defence of Mons and the mining district of the *Borinage* by Field Marshal Sir John French's British Expeditionary Force. Von Kluck advanced at speed westwards, capturing the town of Cambrai until, in early September, his Army had arrived west of Bapaume to form the huge salient in the region of the Somme. Its furthest point was across the River Ancre and 2,000 yards west of Serre onto the Hébuterne-Colincamps Plain.[i] Elsewhere, battle raged on the Marne, the Aisne and in Flanders.

Generaloberst
Alexander von Kluck.

The German, French and British front lines for 1914, 1915 and 1916 had been established in those early days of September.

Cambrai was a city with a population of about 28,000, connected by good roads and a railway network to all parts of the German line on the Western Front; and back into the German heartland, the Ruhr and major cities. With its plentiful accommodation, warehouses and large buildings - not to mention the

Ruins of Cambrai Church.

available French workforce - the town became the Germans' most important base in the north. Situated in open rolling farming land at least forty miles from the battle front, it was a peaceful place, disturbed only slightly by reconnaissance aircraft. The area around the city was where battered divisions were brought to rest, recover and re-equip. It became known as the 'Flanders Sanatorium'.

General Sir Douglas Haig took over command of the BEF in December 1915; he was aware of Cambrai's significance. However he was occupied enough with places much closer to the line than Cambrai, so that an attack on it was something for the future, a hoped for possibility. After the summer and autumn months of 1916 and the terrible Battle of the Somme, Erich Ludendorff, effectively in command of the German army, decided to extricate his badly damaged army from the Somme and to build a new line to the rear, thereby reducing the frontage and improving the lines of communication. Therefore he ordered the *Siegfried Stellung* to be constructed, the strongest defensive line the modern world had ever seen.

Prince Rupprecht.   Erich Ludendorff.

The new forty-five mile line stretched south easterly from Arras and in front of Cambrai. The British called it the Hindenburg Line.[ii] In late February 1917 the Germans, under the command of Prince Rupprecht of Bavaria, began their

A medical detachment retreats back towards the Hindenburg Line.

A road near Havrincourt Wood blocked by the Germans.

withdrawal. This was carefully planned, fighting for almost every mile, and exacting heavy casualties on General Sir Henry Rawlinson's Fourth Army as it followed them towards Cambrai. Instructions had ordered the devastation of every village, wood, road, culvert and well – anything that might be of value to the Allies – in a most savage 'scorched earth' policy. So extreme was this policy that Prince Rupprecht almost resigned when the extent of what was proposed was revealed to him, but he was persuaded of its necessity.

Ludendorff's *Siegfried Stellung* obviously had to be completed in order to receive the withdrawing troops behind it. The great defence lines consisted of many rows of deep trenches – each protected by rows (some were twenty or more yards wide) of heavy gauge barbed wire – dug purposely very deep and wide to prevent tanks crossing and all with strong dugouts and positions for machine guns. Every isolated farmhouse was turned into a fortress.

The strongest part of the whole system, five miles deep with six major lines, was in front of Cambrai. The system here used part of the

A segment of the Hindenburg Line, illustrating the massive barbed wire defences.

Canal du Nord, under construction before the war commenced, but not completed: it was dug but dry. It lay six miles west of the town, running round the eastern edge of the 2,000 acre Havrincourt Wood and then headed north to connect with the River Sensée. Six miles south west of Cambrai is the village of Ribécourt, which sits in the middle of a twenty square mile shallow 'bowl'. Two miles north of that village is the upper edge of the area, Flesquières Ridge. The village of Havrincourt is two miles west of Flesquières, at the end of the ridge and a few hundred yards from the (then) dry canal. From there the line followed the western edge of the Trescault Ridge, heading south to the southern rim of the 'bowl'. This was formed by the Bonavis Ridge, from Gonnelieu to Banteux. Banteux lies alongside the fully functioning St Quentin Canal, which is situated in a valley five miles from Trescault. The canal is sixty feet wide and ten feet deep and formed the eastern edge of the 'bowl' and the *Siegfried Stellung*.

The canal passes through six villages in its route towards Cambrai, each with a steel road or railway bridge. At Crèvecoeur it turns sharply to the west; after a mile or so it flows through Masnières and after another mile the canal turns sharply to the north at Marcoing to continue on, running through the western suburb of Cambrai until it reaches the River Sensée, five miles north of the city. The area described is the 'bowl'; the heart of the 'Flanders Sanatorium', and the defences for Cambrai. Dominating the whole, three miles west of the town, on the north side of the ancient Roman road connecting Cambrai to Bapaume and half a mile beyond the village of Fontaine Notre Dame, is the wooded, 640 acre, 150 feet high Bourlon Hill. Just behind it, on the north side, is the village of Bourlon.

Now that the Germans had withdrawn so close to Cambrai, Haig could see that there were strategic possibilities here. But he had already determined his priority for 1917 – and that action would take place in Flanders, before Ypres. In May 1917 the Field Marshal discussed with Byng (Third Army) and Rawlinson (Fourth Army) the possibilities of offensive action at Cambrai; but no plans were made. In June Sir Henry Rawlinson's Fourth Army went up to the Belgian coast and was relieved by Third Army. Sir Julian Byng was then invited (in the utmost secrecy) to produce a plan for an

11

Sir Julian Byng.

Sir Henry Rawlinson.

attack on this part of the Hindenburg Line - but at this stage it was to be no more than a plan, only known of by his immediate staff.

Haig had, amongst others, two brilliant, innovative and enthusiastic specialists in his command. The first was Brigadier General H.H. Tudor (a gunner), the artillery commander of the 9th (Scottish) Division. He appreciated what the German artillery expert, Lieutenant Colonel Bruchmüller, had accomplished at Riga (on the Eastern Front) by the use of unregistered shooting. This meant the elimination of the usual method of registering targets by preliminary shooting that preceded the customary long bombardment. This was achieved by the use of the technology that the war had spawned – aerial reconnaissance and photography, sound ranging and flash spotting. The traditional method doubtless caused some casualties, but was a clear indication to the enemy that an offensive was planned and allowed them time to take counter measures. The traditional method was what had happened on 1 July on the Somme; at a time when the Royal Artillery was too inexperienced to use anything else; and before some of these technical innovations had been developed. In addition, it was intended to do away with any form of preliminary bombardment to soften up the enemy defences or to destroy their heavier artillery. Tudor prepared an artillery plan accordingly.

Brigadier General H. H. Tudor.

The other officer was Brigadier General H.J. Elles, a forty year old sapper, who had been selected by Haig in 1915 to be one of those to investigate the possibilities of what became the tank. Hugh Elles had gathered round him other enthusiasts: Major Martel, Captains Uzuelli, Tapper and Hotblack, and others who were dedicated to turning the Heavy Branch Machine Gun Corps into a battle-winning – even war-winning - formation. Elles established a forty acre depot at Bermicourt, west of Arras, near St Pol. He was determined to improve the image of the badly designed, unreliable machine that had seen action in the autumn of 1916 and at Arras in the spring of 1917 into one in which the infantry could

Brigadier General H. J. Elles.

12

have confidence. On 27 July 1917 the Heavy Branch had become the Tank Corps, with its own cap badge. The planning the two brigadier generals commenced in the summer of 1917 would begin to revolutionise the way the army fought land battles.

In the same period, Crown Prince Rupprecht (commander of the Caudry Group of Armies) met the German Second Army's commander, General von der Marwitz, at the latter's Headquarters in Le Cateau to discuss what strength was required in front of Cambrai, within the *Siegfried Stellung*. They were convinced that the *Siegfried Stellung* was invincible. By early November the line was held by only three divisions. The 20th Landwehr (Lieutenant General Freiherr von Hanstein) held the front from Moeuvres, a mile north of the Cambrai to Bapaume road south to Havrincourt. On its

General von der Marwitz.

left, from Havrincourt down to the Bonavis Ridge at La Vacquerie, a six mile front, was the 54th Infantry Division (Lieutenant General Freiherr von Watter), which arrived in the sector in August, battle weary from Ypres. Below the 54th, on the southern side of Bonavis Ridge, was Lieutenant General Hildermann's 9th Reserve Division. Rupprecht's only defence at the western edge of the 'bowl' facing Trescault was the tired 54th with not much artillery, 34 guns, (consisting of some howitzers and 77mm field pieces) and a battery of heavy mortars. It was also short of ammunition. However it was thought to be certainly enough to stop any initial attack – an attack which Rupprecht could not see happening.

In the early autumn Brigadier General Elles started to gather his tanks together, many of which were recovered from the battlefields. He welcomed the arrival of the new MK IV and pursued the recruitment and training of crews. Planning for the offensive continued, but nothing

Almost certainly G78 (2/Lt Leek's) tank, ditched north of Graincourt.

could be done whilst the Third Battle of Ypres continued.

As the fighting at Ypres became reduced to ensuring a tenable winter line, Sir Douglas Haig saw the opportunity of advancing north from Cambrai to move behind the River Sensée, getting behind the German lines and cutting their troops off from their supply bases. He was also acutely aware of the Russian Front collapsing, thus releasing battle hardened German divisions for use on the Western Front.

On 13 October Haig approved Sir Julian Byng's plan, which remained cloaked in secrecy. It was only on 26 October that Byng could confide his battle plan to all of his Headquarters Staff - everything must be done to avoid the enemy learning what was about to befall them.

However on the evening of the 26th the consequences of the disaster of Caporetto, in Italy, on the BEF was made clear. During this engagement, over eighteen days, the Austro-Hungarian Army and six German divisions routed the Italian Second Army and caused, in one way or another, 650,000 casualties, 250,000 of whom were prisoners. The retreat continued for sixty miles, but the front had been stabilised by 12 November. On 26 October Haig received instructions to despatch troops and artillery to the Italian Front. Sir Douglas Haig was now in a dilemma. About to embark on Cambrai, his divisions short of men, the War Cabinet now called upon him to send four divisions with artillery and aircraft to Italy, two of them to go immediately. General Plumer (Second Army), who was fighting at Ypres, would command the force.

Haig argued that, to avoid the possibility of German divisions released from the Russian Front (and, indeed, from the end of the fighting at Ypres) being directed to Italy and to the French sector in the south, he should begin his Cambrai offensive. Consequently, he argued, in a letter of 10 November to General Sir William Robertson, the Chief of the Imperial General Staff, that the Ypres operation should cease except for artillery bombardments for another fortnight (as arranged), to stop the enemy from denuding the front. They might then consider that this was only a lull in the battle, as had occurred, for example, in September. He went on to argue that the Third Army offensive must carry on (ie Cambrai) as this would be the best way of helping

General Sir William Robertson.

both the Italians and the French. He hoped that this would stop the further two divisions (and artillery and aircraft) from going to Italy, as promised by the War Cabinet. On 15 November he wrote to say that the new offensive could be stopped if it appeared to entail greater losses than he could afford.

The Field Marshal decided that the middle of November had to be the time, not least if tanks were going to be used and action taken before winter set in. Suffice to say for this volume, six divisions would attack into the 'bowl', the German 54th Division's sector. There would be four from III Corps (6th, 12th, 20th and 29th) which would go for the St Quentin Canal and its bridges. Two from IV Corps (51st and 62nd) would strike north eastwards over the Flesquières Ridge and into the German 20th Landwehr Division's sector. Their objectives were the four villages in front of Bourlon Hill three miles away, the hill itself and Bourlon village beyond it. The attack by the six divisions would be followed by Lieutenant General Sir C.T. Kavanagh's Cavalry Corps, which would encircle Cambrai from the south and cut it off from reinforcements.

The infantry offensive commenced at exactly the same time as 1,000 guns began their unregistered shoot. 476 tanks, 378 of them fighting tanks, went forward and 289 aircraft took off over the front line. All of this started at 6.20 a.m. on 20 November. The target for completion of this stupendous operation was daybreak on the 21st - only twenty-four hours. However, all did not go according to plan. The story of the preparations for the battle, the battle itself, and the defence of the ground gained by the divisions of III Corps against the German counter offensive is told in the authors' *Cambrai: The Right Hook*, in this series. It is recommended that it be read first. The story of the protracted and difficult battle of the 51st (Highland) Division at Flesquières, because of the wealth of detail, will be told in a further volume. When the battle finally ended on 7 December both sides were tired out and had suffered almost equal casualties: the Germans 53,000 from twenty divisions, without tanks; the British 47,000 from fifteen infantry and four cavalry divisions and three brigades of tanks. Of these there were approximately 6,000 British prisoners and 11,000 German. Cambrai, captured in September 1914, would remain in German hands until September 1918.

---

i. For further details about the actions around Serre, see *Serre* in this series.
ii. *The Hindenburg Line* in this series gives fuller details, especially of those parts of it which have survived to the present day.

Acknowledgements

I am indebted to all those who have laboured before me in researching and recording what went on in those days at the end of November and early December 1917 in the attack on the Hindenburg Line and Cambrai. Above all, I owe much to the authors of regimental histories and the compilers of the War Diaries and Volume III, 1917 of the *Official History: France and Flanders,* by Captain Wilfrid Miles. I wish to thank Nigel Cave whose encouragement, unstinting help and friendship (with complete access to his remarkable library) was so fundamental to my ever contemplating writing this guide. He has taught me that, even at seventy-eight, it is never too old to learn. My grateful thanks go to the remarkable gentleman, author and hotelier in Cambrai, Philippe Gorczynski, who seems to know more about the tank battles at Cambrai than anyone else. He spent much time showing me so many places and things, driving me around the area in his 4x4 vehicle, including the seemingly impenetrable Bourlon Wood to find long hidden memorials and German bunkers which I would never have otherwise seen.

My gratitude is also due to Steve Gough, cartographer of the Western Front Association; and the staff at the Commonwealth War Graves Commission in Maidenhead, who never failed to provide details of war cemeteries and information about those buried or commemorated there, in particular the recipients of the Victoria Cross who lie in their care. Last, but not least, as ever I am grateful to all at Pen and Sword: Brigadier Henry Wilson, the Publishing Manager, and the Wilkinson father and sons team who turn all the works into such splendid volumes.

The following books were particularly useful in the compilation of this guide:

Military Operations France and Belgium, 1917, Vol III, compiled by CaptainWilfrid Miles MC

History of the 40th Division, Lieutenant Colonel F.E.Whitton CMG.

History of the 4th Seaforth Highlanders, Lieutenant Colonel M.M. Haldane.

The Iron Clads of Cambrai, Bryan Cooper.

A Wood Called Bourlon, William Moore.

Fields of Death, Peter Slowe and Richard Woods.

History of the Royal Tank Regiment, George Forty.

Following The Tanks at Cambrai, Jean-Luc Gibot and Philippe Gorczynski.

16

Advice for Tourers

This very important battlefield is only about thirty minutes from Bapaume; the good, straight road to Cambrai, the N30, runs through it. It is about eighty miles from Calais and connected by autoroutes. I suspect the few visitors it gets arrive at the daunting bulk of Bourlon Wood and, after a drive up its western side to Bourlon village and a stroll up the hill into the wood to look at the Military Cemetery and the Canadian Memorial, it is all the majority see. In fact it is a most interesting, extensive, yet compact battlefield, with so much hardly changed in all the years. The country is really beautiful, dotted with a number of sleepy villages which all feature in the battle scene. Because of the good access to it, a tour of the rest of the Cambrai battlefield may easily be combined with the five tours of the southern half of the Battle of Cambrai, covered in the authors' *Cambrai: The Right Hook*. In addition, because of its proximity to Bapaume, a tour of the Somme battlefields between there and Albert can easily be added to a stay in the area. However, I would suggest that with this guide you will find several days can be fully filled here.

Accommodation is varied, plentiful and usually good. You will find a suggested list at the end of this section. The standard travel advice regarding vehicle and personal insurance is offered – ie make sure that

Bourlon church today and a picture of the explosion when the Germans removed the spire to prevent it being used as an aiming point. Philippe Gorczynski

you are covered. Ensure your Europe breakdown cover is adequate and that the Form E111 for reciprocal medical care is fully completed. The necessities for a picnic lunch are plentiful in the village shops (as well as in supermarkets on the edge of Cambrai), but bring a bottle opener, corkscrew and drinking mugs. Films are generally cheaper in the UK. Do not forget the legal essentials for your car, two warning triangles, a first aid kit and a set of spare bulbs; and a tow rope and an empty petrol can, just in case. The maps and directions in the guide should be sufficient but it is strongly recommended to obtain the Green Series (1:100000) No 4 map – Laon Arras. This excellent map for navigation purposes covers both the Cambrai and Somme battlefields (and all but the northernmost part of the Arras one as well). The most recent Blue Series maps 2507 East and West, 1:25,000 are also recommended. The tours (except for inside Bourlon Wood) are not difficult; but good walking shoes are recommended and rubber boots if the weather has been particularly inclement. A rucksack to hold everything (including some binoculars), with some wet weather gear and a plastic bag for muddy boots are a good idea. Please be aware of the owners' land and property and do not leave your vehicle blocking gates, tracks or paths. The land has been almost entirely cleared of munitions but some remain and if you find any leave them well alone.

Bourlon Wood is an exception to this – although cleared to a degree, the action of tree roots and the nature of the ground means that munitions of all types are likely to be found here. A venture into the wood is not for the faint hearted. The few paths, 'rides', are deeply rutted and winding – and are definitely not for vehicles. They go over sharply rolling hillside, densely covered with undergrowth and fallen trees: movement off the rides should not be made – amongst other things this is private property. It should also be noted that many of the rides are themselves private, though it is a little difficult to know which is 'communal' and which is not. The atmosphere within it is heavy - almost frightening - with the closely packed trees and deep hollows, some of which have deep pools hiding many things. There are still hundreds of projectiles deep in the soft undergrowth, and the ground certainly holds the remains of many men of both sides. For some years after the war the stench was formidable; several times searches were made, sinking long rods into the ground to try and locate the missing. In early 2001, whilst working to extract timber, a tractor struck a German phosgene gas shell and released a great cloud of poison gas. The driver was rushed to hospital but recovered after several days there. However, to go inside the wood, as the tour suggests, is an experience not forgotten. It is difficult to imagine how men could ever have fought or even maintained contact in such awful conditions - and you will have been in there only in daylight. Do not, under any circumstances, use a metal detector. Be conscious that this wood is used for hunting – therefore be aware of the breeding period and be extremely cautious during the long hunting season itself: the weekends are particularly dangerous, but hunting can take place on any day!

The wood is private property, owned in large part (but not exclusively) by the elderly and charming Comte Pierre de Francqueville, who lives in Abbey Farm on the northern edge of the wood, adjacent to the British Military Cemetery.

Accommodation.

There are many hotels in Cambrai. *The Hotel Beatus*, on the St Quentin road, five hundred yards from the old Paris gate, (718 Avenue de Paris, 59400 Cambrai, Tel: (00 33 3) 27.81.45.70. Fax: 27.78.00.83.) is highly recommended. If you are lucky the owner, Philippe Gorczynski, might volunteer to take you into Bourlon Wood.

Fontaine Notre Dame: actually the hotels below are just by the autoroute interchange, on the western edge of Cambrai.
Hotel Ibis, Route de Bapaume 59400 Fontaine, Tel: 3.27.82.99.88. Fax: 3.27.82.99.88
Hotel Campanile, Route de Bapaume, Tel: 3.27.81.62.00.
There are many others as you enter the town.

Accommodation on the Somme:
Avril Williams Guest House, 10 Rue Delattre, 80560 Auchonvillers, Tel: +33.322.76.23.66
Julie Renshaw, Les Galets, 80560 Auchonvillers, Tel: +33.322.76.28.79.
Hotel De La Paix, Bapaume 62450 Tel: +33.321.07.11.03.

Accommodation in the southern sector:
Ferme des Escarts, Les Rue de Vignes, 59241 Masnières Tel: +33.327.37.51.10.

There are many more in this area, a number of which may be found in *Cambrai: The Right Hook.*

LIST OF MAPS

Tanks carrying fascines, to fill in trenches to facilitate crossing deep trenches. Pictured are tanks of 'C' Battalion, commanded by Lt. Col S H Charrington. Tank C22, 'Cynic', was commanded by 2/Lt D. F. Brundrit.

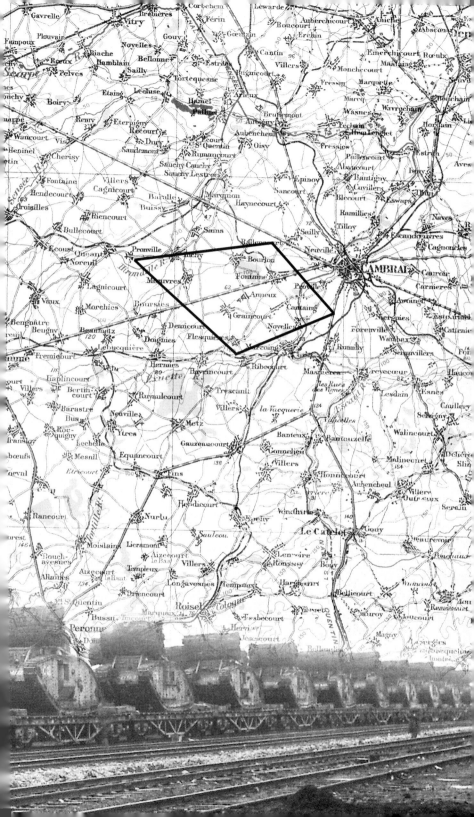

CAMBRAI 1917
SITUATION 20 NOVEMBER

British Front at zero hour	-------
British Front at nightfall	———
Corps boundary	- - - - -
Defensive flank	-·-·-·-
Hindenburg system	Green

Heights in metres

Scale: 0 1000 2000 3000 4000 5000 6000
yards

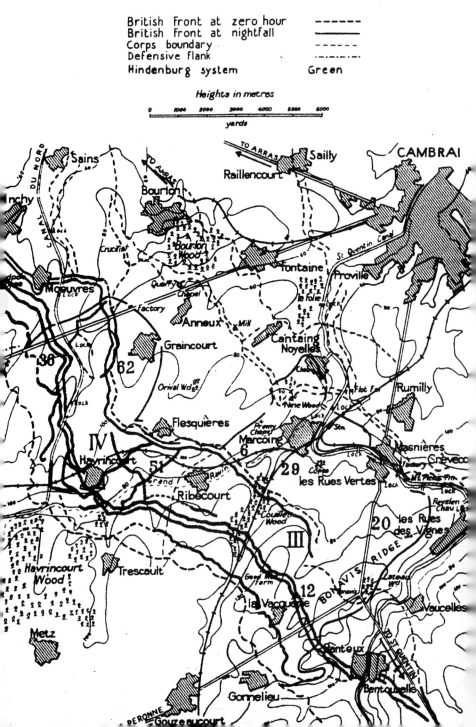

Chapter One

SETTING THE SCENE

The morning of 21 November was cold, wet, murky and miserable, but in London and throughout Great Britain church bells rang, the first time since the beginning of the war, to celebrate the victorious advance to the St Quentin Canal of III Corps. All the men of those four divisions and the two of IV Corps were tired and hungry after their four miles deep penetration into the German lines over a six mile front. Such a spectacular advance had not previously been seen on the Western Front - and at a cost of only 4,000 casualties. Almost 200 of the 374 tanks that had been committed were out of action; and after a further twelve hours of daylight battle many more were desperately in need of maintenance and repair. The crews, whose accepted length of continuous battlefield duty in the cordite and exhaust fume-filled machine was eight hours, were exhausted, some physically sick, a lot of them wounded and yet still fighting their boiling hot tanks. The two attacking divisions of Lieutenant General Sir Charles Woollcombe's IV Corps, the 62nd (2nd West Yorkshire) Division and the 51st (Highland) Division had cleared the Flesquières Ridge. The 62nd had done extremely well and were now at Graincourt, a large village 7,000 yards north of the start line. The West Yorkshire battalions of 185 Brigade and the King's Own Yorkshire Light Infantry and the York and Lancaster men of 187 Brigade had come out of Havrincourt Wood and crossed the hundred feet wide and twenty feet deep dry ditch of the Canal Du Nord in four hours against strong resistance; they took more

Tanks pass by a captured 77mm field gun at Graincourt. The tank is probably 'Gorgonzola' II G29. 2/Lt A. G. Baker, commanding, was awarded a bar to his MC in the battle

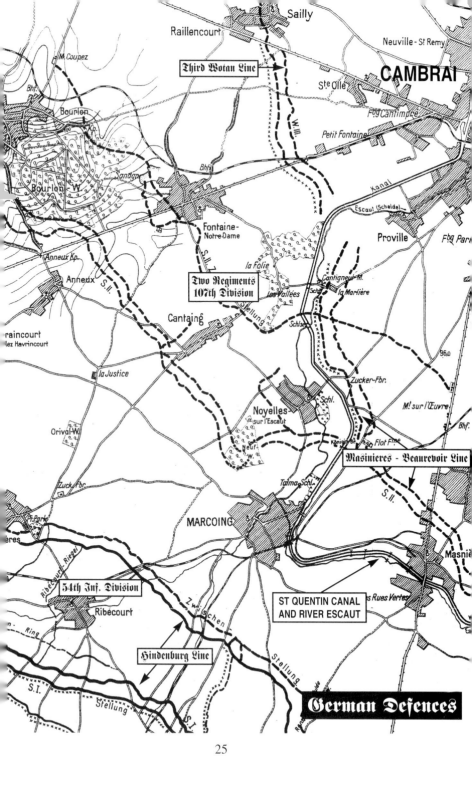

General R.B. 'Boy' Bradford VC MC.

than 1,000 prisoners from the German 54th Division. The 2/6th West Yorks were particularly badly hit, losing seven officers and 150 other ranks in the attack on Havrincourt Chateau; but by 10.15am the village was taken. At 9am 186 Brigade, consisting of Territorials from the Duke of Wellington's Regiment, came out of Havrincourt Wood to take up the Division's advance. The Brigade was commanded by the youngest general in the British Army (aged 25). Brigadier General R.B. 'Boy' Bradford VC MC, who had won the Victoria Cross whilst commanding two battalions of the Durham Light Infantry near Le Sars, at Eaucourt l'Abbaye in October 1916. However it was not until 3.30pm, because of fierce resistance, that the Dukes came through the almost undamaged Graincourt and prepared to go for the smaller village of Anneux, 1,000 yards to the north-east. Bradford, in the front with his lead battalion, the 2/4th Dukes, got to the Bapaume-Cambrai road and secured the Sugar Factory, some 3,000 yards east of a destroyed bridge at the dry canal. Because it was now dark and the road and Anneux were obviously heavily wired and strongly defended, he withdrew into Graincourt. His venture beyond that village had been full of adventure, taking troops of the 20th Landwehr Division by surprise. A long column of them, marching unawares towards Cambrai, was attacked and the British captured an officer and three men from the tail of the column and killed or wounded about eighty others. The 2/4th Dukes had suffered only fifty three casualties during its advance earlier in the morning; however at Havrincourt the 2/5th Battalion had lost its Commanding Officer (Lieutenant Colonel T.A.D. Best) and 72 other men. With his Brigade in and about Graincourt, Bradford located his HQ in the crypt of the Church. The 62nd Division at dawn on the 21st prepared to go forward with the assistance of some tanks and dismounted cavalry. The cavalrymen had taken part on the first day but, without a breakthrough, horses had no place on the battlefield faced with uncut wire and machine guns.

The 51st (Highland) Division had fought bitterly and with difficulty for Flesquières. Their problems were in part due to Major General Harper's dislike of the suggested method of operating with tanks and both the infantry and tanks suffered many casualties. Lance Corporal R. McBeath of the 1/5th Seaforth's won his Victoria Cross advancing to the village. The full story of this action will be told in a future volume in this series. Nevertheless, shortly after daybreak the Division

26

Lance Corporal R. McBeath VC.

had got clear of the village and was looking at the mist shrouded Bourlon Hill almost three miles north across the open, practically treeless, plain and with a bitterly cold wind blowing in their faces.

A third division of General Woollcombe's IV Corps (whose HQ was fifteen miles to the west at Villers-au-Flos) the 36th (Ulster) Division (Major General O.S.W. Nugent) had started out at 8.35am, on the western side of the dry canal, with three Brigades: 107 and 108 in reserve, and 109 advancing. After a minor skirmish it had arrived at the Demicourt-Graincourt road within three hours and the 9/Royal Inniskilling Fusiliers took over the lead. By nightfall the Division had crossed the road and had got into the northward running *Siegfried Stellung*, near to the destroyed bridge on the main road. Its orders for the 21st was to seize the area of the damaged bridge, to advance north to Moeuvres, a 3,000 yard jump, and to take Inchy, a further 3,000 yard jump, as soon as Bourlon village had fallen. The purpose of this was to secure the left flank of the attack. It was a formidable task but Moeuvres had to be taken by dawn, a village well into the zone of the 20th Landwehr Division, General Bellman's territory.

On the far left flank, north of the main road at Boursies, and a mile west of the canal was the fourth division of IV Corps, the 56th (1st London) Division (Major General F.A. Dudgeon). It would work north through the German lines and enter Moeuvres from the west. Then all would be set for the attack on Bourlon.

What had happened to the German defenders? The 54th Infantry and the 20th Landwehr Divisions (along with a regiment of the 107th Division) had almost been destroyed by nightfall - 159 officers and 7,316 other ranks had become prisoners alone - but Rupprecht, surprised at the British attack and its success, quickly brought in reinforcements in the early hours of the 21st. General Brauchitsch's 214th Infantry Division came first, followed by the 30th Infantry Division (General Lambsdorff). By the morning of the 22nd the 119th Infantry Division and General Lindequist's 3rd Guards would be at Cambrai, with seven others warned to be ready. All of these incoming divisions were fresh troops, whilst the British were tired and depleted.

The task for IV Corps was going to be formidable, made worse by the great difficulty, due to distance and the wrecked roads, deep in mud, of getting artillery forward. There was one other factor at dawn on the 21st which concerned the Field Marshal. The target time for completion of the operation was twenty-four hours; the time was up. He had said at the outset he would close the battle down if its objectives had not been achieved within forty-eight hours. He would wait on events and until later in the day before he decided what to do.

Chapter Two

THE ADVANCE TO BOURLON
21st to 22nd of November

General Braithwaite's 62nd Division, on the left of the 51st, was positioned in and behind Graincourt, its great caves housing most of it. The attack line of both divisions faced north-east. General Harper's lay over the ridge, on the north eastern edge of Flesquières, between the sugar factory on the Cantaing road and Orival Wood, 1000 yards towards Graincourt.

The objectives were, for the 62nd, the village of Anneux 1,500 yards

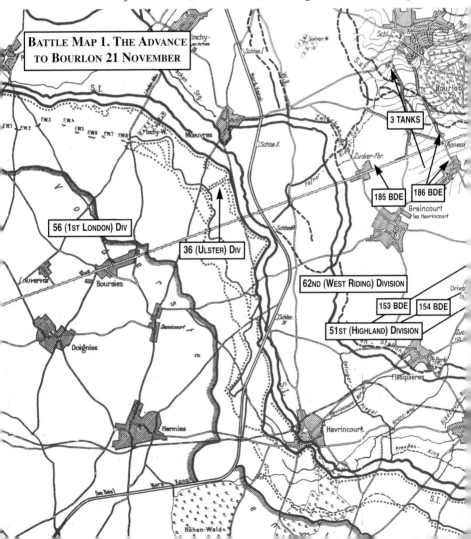

BATTLE MAP 1. THE ADVANCE TO BOURLON 21 NOVEMBER

German soldiers in Anneux after the battle.

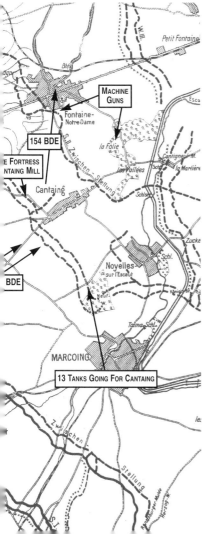

away and then, 500 yards beyond it, the double trenches of the Canting Line. This was an extension (or switch) of the Masnières - Beaurevoir Line, and went for 3,000 yards north along the western edge of the strongly wired Bourlon Hill, as far as the crucifix, 900 yards south-west of Bourlon village on the road to Moeuvres. It then continued for a further 2,000 yards north-westerly to Quarry Wood. When this was achieved, the 62nd Division would sweep westwards and take the whole of Bourlon village. The Division expected to have twenty tanks by about 10am and some cavalry provided by the 11th Hussars and King Edward's Horse. It was a truly formidable task, which had to be undertaken by tired men.

General Harper's 51st Division had the most important role. It would attack north-easterly towards Cantaing, 3,000 yards away. Its first objective was the sunken

Premy Chapel-Graincourt road, halfway across the open, shallowly rolling land, then Cantaing, situated behind a double line of partially completed trenches - though already strongly wired. The position had many machine gun emplacements. When that was secured it would advance to the larger, long, straggling village of Fontaine Notre Dame, a total advance of 6,000 yards. Tanks had been promised for 10am. Lieutenant A. Macdonnel, an artillery liaison officer with the Seaforths described the scene that morning as an astonishing sight, tanks advancing in waves and cavalry with drawn sabres. The Highlanders set off first after an artillery bombardment, two battalions each from the 153rd on the left of the 152nd Brigade, 1/6th Black Watch and 1/5th Gordons and the 1/5th Seaforths and 1/8th Argylls on the Division's right flank. There was some desultory machine gun and rifle opposition, but by 9am a 2,000 yard length of the road was held. They had captured seventy Germans and twelve field guns. On the right the Seaforths of 152 Brigade had pushed forward towards Cantaing but were stopped by heavy machine gun fire. In and about the village were two Reserve Regiments of General Havenstein's 107th Infantry Division, the 52nd and 232nd, who had been rushed into position during the night. Brigadier General Buchanan's 154 Brigade now pushed through to lead the advance on Cantaing. His attack was scheduled to start at 10am and the lead battalions, 1/4th Gordons and 1/7th Argylls, halted at the captured road to wait for the tanks. Lieutenant Colonel Rowbotham (only 26 years old), commanding the Gordons, actually led his Battalion on horseback. He would be awarded the DSO for his work that day. It was still raining, which helped the attack as it obscured it from the enemy observers on Bourlon Hill. The tanks, about six, only arrived at noon; supported by the guns of LXX Field Battery, Buchanan's 154 Brigade went forward at 10.30 am, as he could not afford to wait. At first they were held up by wire and machine guns, but with the help of the tanks (when they eventually arrived) the Gordons were able to get ahead with speed. Despite the enemy's resistance, most of Cantaing quickly fell; but the enemy were not giving it up so easily and a pocket of them were not cleared out until 3.30pm, 300 prisoners being taken. Five hundred yards

Brigadier General Buchanan.

Cantaing – left middle distance, Cambrai – right far distance. In the foreground is a German defensive work dug by forced civilian labours.

north of Cantaing, on the track to Anneux, was the Mill, converted into a fortress with two 77mm field guns and numerous machine guns. That, and the other defences in the Cantaing Line, brought the Highlanders to a halt. The cavalry, a dismounted squadron of the Queen's Bays (though they had arrived on horseback), could do nothing. Flying low overhead were enemy aircraft, machine gunning the prone troops. Lieutenant Colonel J.S. Unthank's 1/4th Seaforths had now come forward on the left of the Brigade but could not advance through the belts of wire. Sergeant A. Ross of No 1 Company was sent forward with half a dozen men to silence a particularly menacing machine gun nest. Although he could not get at it (he was wounded in the attempt) his rifle fire drove the Germans back into the village and put one of the guns out of action. At the end of the battle he was awarded the DCM. At midday the Division was dug in and stuck, unable to make further progress. Soon afterwards thirteen tanks came over the Premy Chapel ridge, about a mile to the south, followed by a company of the DLI, who broke into the wire there. By this time Battalion HQ of the 1/4th was forward at the farmhouse of La Justice, 800 yards behind the lead companies. Two of these advanced behind the tanks, two of which were knocked out by German gunners. Captain T.D. Raike's tank had 43 bullet holes in it. By 1.30pm the village was cleared of the enemy, but casualties were high. Unthank's men had conquered the Mill, 400 prisoners were taken and the survivors of the German 52nd and 232nd Regiments withdrew behind the Wotan III Sunken Switch Line into La Folie Wood and Fontaine. They reported a very trying day. They had fought the tanks valiantly, without armour piercing ammunition, engaging them over open sights with field guns. Nevertheless the enemy's trials for the day were not yet over - nor were the Highlanders'. General Harper had issued orders that nothing more must be attempted; but Buchanan's men were going forward, 'their blood was up'. The 1/7th Argylls and the 1/4th Seaforths, advancing

This ditched tank on the road west of Fontaine Notre Dame is NO. H48, Hypatia, commanded by 2/Lt B.O. Hancock. Philippe Gorczynski

behind four tanks, were killing or capturing many Germans as they sought to get into Fontaine, more than a mile away. In the late afternoon, as darkness was falling, the tanks, crews exhausted and low on ammunition, smashed forward through the barbed wire in front of Fontaine, killing and silencing the line of machine guns on its southern

British graves in Orival Wood, the basis of the current CWGC cemetery.

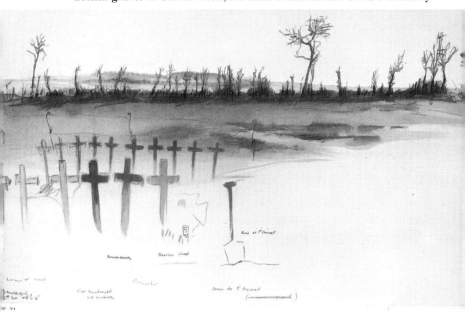

edge. They cruised through the village. At 5.15pm, almost out of ammunition they turned around and headed for home, satisfied that the defenders had all fled. The two Highland Battalions remained in the village to winkle out the Germans hiding there. The 1/7th Argylls, despite their casualties, headed for the north-eastern side of Fontaine. They had to push through the civilian village population, who had come out of hiding with bottles of wine to greet the *Ecossais*. The Seaforths advance had not been easy. Captain Macdonald's company, following the tanks, was struck by heavy fire on the edge of the village and the Captain was mortally wounded. His body was later recovered and taken back to be buried in Orival Wood. The Battalion kept going until it too was at the far end of the village, digging in across the exit road to Cambrai. The prize was now only 4,000 yards away and ready for the taking. Rupprecht commented later that he was amazed that the British had not continued, as the town would have fallen. However, Byng was far back at Albert (one of the faults in the British organisation was that the commanders were too far away from the battle – though the problem of communications, not surprisingly, made it almost inevitable that senior commanders would be some distance away) was not aware of this, nor did he have the troops to hand. In any case, the plan did not allow for the storming of Cambrai directly – it was to be taken in flank, as street fighting was always expensive in casualties. British casualties at Fontaine were heavy; for example the Seaforths could muster only 120 men. In Captain Macdonald's company, which had started out that morning with 125 officers and men, only 40 were left. The Argylls had just about the same number. The night was quiet, food was sent up, but no ammunition, which they desperately needed. In the quietness of the night, at about 10pm, a horse drawn convoy of German wagons came up towards Fontaine, not suspecting that their men had all left. As it came into the village, the Germans were surprised to find fallen trees blocking the road and drew to a halt. Men of the Seaforths sprang out, grabbing hold of the first wagon, but the others managed to turn around and fled. The two horses were taken back to Flesquières and would be used by the Battalion until the war ended. Later that night the battered Argylls and Gordons were withdrawn to take up a defensive position half way down the main road towards Anneux; their position now looked up at the eastern end of the hill.

The handful of Seaforths was now responsible for the village defences, particularly at the Cambrai end, but the total length of the perimeter they had to guard around Fontaine was 3,500 yards, an impossible task for the few men. There were many Germans licking their wounds in La Folie Wood, less than a mile south of the village. In the distance they could hear trains arriving in Cambrai, the ominous indication of troops being brought in for the morrow. Fortunately the Seaforths C.O., Lieutenant Colonel Unthank, had arrived with his HQ; in the dark he rearranged his men around his defence line, for he knew daylight would bring trouble.

So, what had Major General Braithwaite's Yorkshire men been doing on the 21st? He was still relying on the Dukes in 186 Brigade. As had happened with the Highlanders, his tanks (twenty of them) did not arrive on time; somewhat later nineteen did arrive, but the attack was delayed. The 2/4th Battalion on the Brigade's right advanced with two tanks on Anneux, which was held by a company of the 52nd Reserve Regiment. Five hundred yards north of the village, on the main road, was a small Chapel, just two buildings with a religious shrine, and just beyond it was a quarry. Both of these positions were strongly defended by the 175th Regiment of the German 36th Division. As the Dukes entered Anneux, the enemy occupying the houses poured fire into them from the upper stories. The centre company of the 2/4th had to stop; it would take an hour of fierce fighting before the village was cleared and many of the defenders taken prisoner. The left company moved out of Graincourt against the Sugar Factory on the main road, 600 yards to the north. When the buildings were occupied it turned right to move against the quarry and the Chapel, assisted by a tank. Resistance was soon crushed and it was able to join with the right company in a pincer movement against the village. This right hand company had passed Anneux on the right with the assistance of another

Bourlon Wood photographed from the southwest, late November 1917.

The Sugar Refinery on the Baupaume-Cambrai Road.

tank; the pincer movement helped the main attack on the village to succeed. However, because fire was so intense from Bourlon Wood and the wire extremely thick, nothing more could be done. At midday the Battalion withdrew to a sunken road below Anneux.

The 2/7th Dukes moved out of Graincourt towards the Sugar Factory and at 10am, without tanks, advanced to the north and into a sunken road 1,000 yards up a gradual slope and into the Second Wotan Line of unfinished trenches, but which were strongly wired. Even when the tanks did arrive they could not penetrate the defences and had to stop because of the heavy fire from the slopes of Bourlon Wood. The third battalion engaged in the attack that morning, the 2/6th, was in reserve at Graincourt. With the other two battalions held up it came forward and went to the left of the attack, towards Moeuvres, two miles to the north-west. Before that village they had to negotiate the dry canal, and to the east of that was a part of the Hindenburg Support System, here in the form of a horseshoe of trenches and barbed wire. A tank did not arrive in support until the middle of the afternoon; although the attack against Moeuvres was thwarted, the Dukes had taken possession of part of the Hindenburg Line at a point 700 yards east of the canal on the Havrincourt – Sains-lés-Marquion track. Rupprecht had not been slow in reinforcing his positions, and in this area were the German 386th Regiment and other remnants of the 20th Landwehr Division, along with the 50th Regiment of the 214th Division and two battalions of the 363rd Regiment of the same Division. Though late in coming, the tanks had not been reluctant to press forward. Two or three bravely went up the western slope in the teeth of artillery and machine gun fire and without infantry support, proceeding for about a mile to the crucifix, which was only 900 yards south west of Bourlon village. There one crushed a machine gun nest and others entered into the edge of the wood. Once again, if only there had been more infantry, the village could have fallen. At nightfall Brigadier General Bradford's valiant men withdrew to Graincourt, whilst Brigadier General Viscount Hampden's 185 Brigade took over the front, albeit with some difficulty from the harassing fire. Bradford's Brigade since the outset on the first day had captured more than 1,200 prisoners and 38 guns.

Brigadier-General Viscount Hampden.

IV Corps attack, for the time being, had ended - though Major General Nugent's 36th (Ulster) Division came up during the late afternoon, hoping to get into Moeuvres. They were frustrated by the wire and a strong defence, but succeeded in taking up positions over the main road and at the canal, menacing the village. Major General Dudgeon's 56th (London) Division had also arrived over the road, 2,000 yards west of the blown bridge near Boursies. During the night many civilians, particularly the young, who had been used for forced labour by the Germans, came out of Fontaine and Cantaing. They were helped by British soldiers to bring what belongings they could carry and go behind the British lines, joining the hundreds who had fled the liberated villages along the St Quentin Canal.

The day was not over for Field Marshal Haig. Late that evening, the 21st, he learned of the failure at the St Quentin Canal. His original time limit, a maximum of 48 hours, had almost expired. Therefore he ordered the closing down of the failed battle for the bridges over the canal, the 'Right Hook'. General Woollcombe's IV Corps had not delivered to his expectations either. The problem now was whether to withdraw to a satisfactory position or continue. Certainly Bourlon was within his grasp; this position would not only dominate Cambrai but threaten it from the west. General Robertson had informed him that he could retain the two divisions under orders for Italy and his original reasoning of attracting German divisions to him was still paramount in his thoughts. He was aware, however, that the country and government now expected, indeed needed, a victory, so long in

36

Major General Nugent.

coming. That night he instructed Sir Julian Byng to go for Bourlon with the maximum of effort.

The morning of the 22nd dawned with mist and a cold wind; it would turn to rain in the afternoon. The Seaforths in Fontaine were well aware that they were in a salient and would be at the sharp end of a likely counter attack coming from Cambrai. Unthank had positioned four machine guns in a German trench facing the eastern edge of

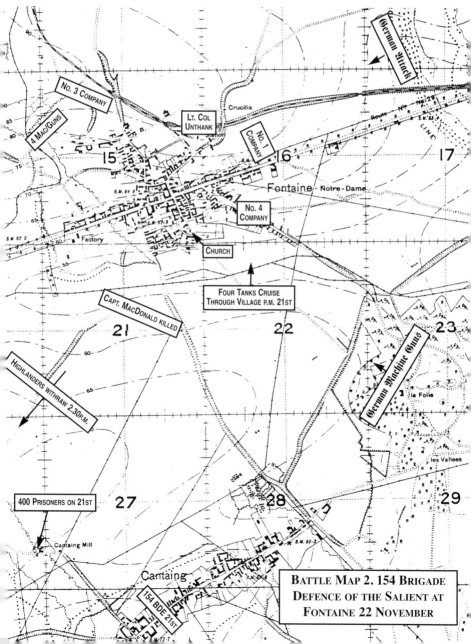

BATTLE MAP 2. 154 BRIGADE DEFENCE OF THE SALIENT AT FONTAINE 22 NOVEMBER

Bourlon Wood; what was left of No. 3 Company went into a small quarry below the railway line on the northern edge of the village; on the right was No.1 Company, north of the main road at the eastern end; No. 2 Company and forty men from No. 4 Company were sent to the south of the eastern exit, looking towards La Folie Wood. A machine gun was put at the western end of the main road and another was positioned to fire across the main road towards La Folie Wood. Battalion HQ was in a house at the crossroads near the church. During the night patrols went out to find the enemy but were unsuccessful. With Germans on three sides, Fontaine was in a very vulnerable position.

The German response started at 6.15am, first light, when numbers of enemy aircraft circled the village until 9am, obviously spotting for the attack; soon afterwards the shelling began. Three German deserters had also arrived who confirmed the presence of the 119th Division; whilst a search of Fontaine's cellars revealed a large number of Germans hoping to evade capture. At 8.30am a messenger had arrived from Brigadier General Buchanan saying that a conference was called for 10am and that the 22nd would be a 'quiet day'. What a forlorn hope for the men in Fontaine; Unthank would have no time to attend it. The enemy could already be seen massing about 1,000 yards away on both sides of the village and the Adjutant, Captain Peverell, sent rockets up, an SOS for artillery support; but owing to the mist they were not seen. The Colonel, with about fifteen men, went up to the railway station a few hundred yards north of the main road. This was fortunate timing, for no sooner had he left the house that he was using as an HQ than it was demolished by a shell. After a desperate fight, by 2.30pm the last few men, now out of ammunition, got clear of the village and crossed the shallow valley to Cantaing, still under machine gun fire. Later, in the dark, the remains of the Battalion got back to Flesquières. The six hours of the Seaforths battle in Fontaine was a time of extraordinary

The streets of Fontaine-Notre-Dame pictured in the early days of the German occupation. Soldiers and civilians standing on the Cambrai-Bapaume Road.

bravery, in which they held off a force of at least regimental strength. There were too many actions to tell in detail here, but a series of sub-headings gives the idea of the ferocity of the battle. The four machine guns facing the eastern edge of Bourlon Wood put out of action within minutes of opening fire, the crews fighting to the death; of the quarry, recaptured by a bayonet charge; of Captain Fraser and four men defending his Company's HQ house until he was killed, and the house captured; of Colonel Unthank who, surrounded, wounded and told to surrender, attacked the six men with a rifle using it like a club, felling them by his ferocity and then escaping; of Captain Green, the Medical Officer, with the Roman Catholic Chaplain, Padre Potter, ordered to leave - which they did reluctantly - but his senior medical NCO, Sergeant Robertson and three others staying behind with the wounded and taken prisoner. For his bravery that day Captain Peverell was recommended for the Victoria Cross (he was captured and later received the DSO). The casualties of the Battalion were eleven officers killed or wounded, thirty other ranks killed, 192 wounded and 86 missing. Much later in December, when the battle at Cambrai was over, the local population said they saw the Germans burning bodies. Despite heroic efforts five days later Fontaine Notre Dame was not recaptured and remained in German hands until September 1918.

What had been happening elsewhere in front of Bourlon Hill on this 'quiet day', 22 November? Many German batteries had been brought up during the 21st on a ten mile arc between Raillencourt, two miles north of Fontaine, and Pronville, a couple of miles west of Moeuvres. Throughout the day they put heavy bombardments on the British line. At 7am Viscount Hampden's 185 Brigade, which had taken over in front of Anneux, received a heavy shelling from both high explosive and gas shells, the 2/6th and 2/8th West Yorks being particularly hit. This was followed by machine gunning from low flying aircraft, and German infantry moving down from Bourlon at midmorning, forcing the Brigade back to the Cambrai road. The 2/6th lost most of its officers and more than a hundred men in the attack. 187 Brigade came to their help at midday, sending in the 2/4th York and Lancs, but the 62nd Division's line, gained only the previous day, was pushed back.

Rupprecht was not yet ready for any major counter attack and was relieved that the British seemed to have abandoned theirs for the time being. He needed this day to get his newly arriving divisions in place, appreciating that the British were no longer interested in capturing Cambrai. He realised that the British thrust would be for Bourlon. When he was ready, in about a week, he would attempt to regain all the lost ground east of the *Siegfried Stellung*. He was content that the British would continue to dissipate their forces against Bourlon – this would leave him less to overcome when the time for his attack came.

Similarly, the tank force was recovering from the first two days. Brigadier General Elles's men were working hard to get them back in action. The MK IV came in two types. The male weighed twenty-eight tons and was twenty-six feet long; it carried two adapted naval six-pounder guns and three (sometimes four) Lewis guns. It would be vital for the next phase of the assault against the concrete bunkers at Bourlon. The female was the same length but narrower (ten feet six inches compared to thirteen feet six inches – it did not need the wide sponsons to carry the guns) - and was equipped only with six

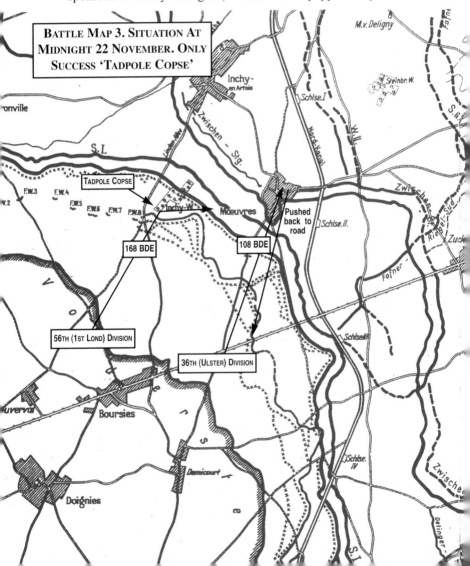

BATTLE MAP 3. SITUATION AT MIDNIGHT 22 NOVEMBER. ONLY SUCCESS 'TADPOLE COPSE'

(sometimes five) Lewis guns for mowing down infantry. The weary crews were getting little or no rest but were eager to attack again; they had seen what their new weapon was capable of achieving. The Germans had also got over the panic of a tank attack. They had soon learnt that the tank was slow – at best it could do a mile an hour over poor going – and cumbersome. The machine was particularly vulnerable if the infantry could be separated from it. The defensive solution was to let the tanks come through before the following up infantry arrived and then attack them with grenades, armour piercing ammunition and 77mm field guns in an anti-tank role. Elles's men were going to have a harder task.

On this 'quiet day' IV Corps artillery (Brigadier General J.G. Geddes) regrouped. Artillery was the crucial weapon in the Great War, and one of the consequences of a big advance was that the guns had to be shifted forward, often over very difficult terrain and using ruined roads. The main problem on the Corps' front was the bottleneck at Havrincourt, a consequence of the dry canal, deep trenches and knee deep mud; but this was overcome and throughout the day the guns combed Bourlon Hill and the village behind with 6" howitzers and 60-pounders. The artillery of the 36th Division supported its resumed attack towards Moeuvres. Little progress was made east of the canal, but the 12th Royal Irish Rifles of 108 Brigade (Brigadier General G.R.J. Griffith) actually entered Moeuvres and penetrated the forward part of the Hindenburg Second Line at the church. But the opposition was too strong either to further the advance or to consolidate the gains and gradually 12/RIR were pushed back to their start point on the Cambrai main road. The 214th Division (the 363rd Regiment) were opposite them and counter attacked from Hobart

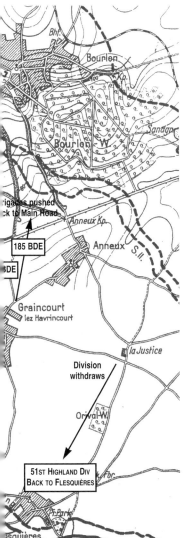

Trench. But the operations on the left flank, facing Bourlon, had not all been a failure. The London Scottish of the 56th Division, despite some heavy shelling by enemy artillery and a counter attack by the 77th Regiment of the 20th Infantry Division, captured Tadpole Copse, a small wood 800 yards west of Moeuvres, situated deep into the Hindenburg Line.

It was not a particularly quiet day for the 40th Division (Major General J. Ponsonby). This was a comparatively new division to the Western Front, which did not arrive there until June 1916, and it missed the awful battles of the Somme. Its first significant actions were in the spring of 1917, at the southern end of the 'Flanders Sanatorium', where it fought against the withdrawing Germans at Beaucamp and Villers Plouich. On 22 November it was brought into IV Corps and arrived at Beaumetz, five miles east of Bapaume, astride the Cambrai road, to the west of the battlefield. At 4pm that day it received orders to relieve the exhausted 62nd Division at Graincourt. Its headquarters were established in Havrincourt (along with its reserve brigade, the 120th (Brigadier General The Honourable C.S.H.D. Willoughby). The other two brigades (119 and 121: Brigadier Generals John Cambell and F. Crozier respectively) pushed on to Graincourt. The relief was not without difficulties as the two available roads and the tracks were not only almost impassable because of mud and shell holes but were also crowded with two way traffic. It took Divisional HQ fifteen hours to cover the nine miles to Havrincourt. The Yorkshire men of the 62nd were not unhappy to come away, to put it mildly. In only two days they had suffered high casualties, 75 officers and 1,613 other ranks. Dawn was breaking before they were clear and had handed over their positions at the main road. This congestion in the whole of IV Corps sector would seriously affect supplies to both the tanks and artillery.

In the morning of the 22nd the Commander-in-Chief, accompanied by his Staff and escort, a cavalcade of about sixty men on horses, rode up to Flesquières Ridge to view the battlefield. He was satisfied with what he saw and that evening he called on Sir Julian Byng in Albert, pointing out that any delay at Bourlon Wood would be unsatisfactory. The War Cabinet was not being particularly helpful to Douglas Haig, its reluctance even now to send him the reinforcements he needed was of great anxiety.

At daybreak on the 23rd both sides were apprehensive; the British, perhaps, more than the Germans. Rupprecht had many more divisions on their way to the Cambrai front.

Chapter Three

THE BATTLE FOR BOURLON WOOD AND VILLAGE
23rd - 26th November

The plan for the capture of Bourlon was finalised. The attack would take place along the whole of the slightly curved 10,000 yard front. On the left the 56th Division would advance north-westwards up to and beyond Tadpole Copse, a long narrow wood 1,000 yards west of Moeuvres. On its right the 36th Division would advance north on both sides of the (dry) Canal Du Nord, through the Hindenburg and Wotan Lines and capture Sains-lès-Marquion, two and a half miles north of Moeuvres. The 40th Division, now in place, would capture Bourlon Hill and village whilst the 51st would retake Fontaine and push north to take the eastern side of Bourlon village. When these tasks were achieved the 1st Cavalry Division (Major General R.L. Mullens) would advance through Fontaine to the railway north-west of Raillencourt, thus cutting off any of the enemy between it and Bourlon. Artillery support would be strong, some seventy batteries with at least thirty-eight heavy guns, 9.2" and 12" calibre, and others. It was hoped to have ninety-two tanks available, thirty-six to advance with the 51st Division, thirty-two with the 40th Division and twelve with the 36th Division. To

Bourlon Wood. Looking north over the Cambrai-Bapaume Road. The Sugar factory is on the left. Buildings on the right mark Anneux cross roads. The length of road between the buildings was the scene of the 2/4 Dukes ambush of the German column from the 20th Landwehr Division.

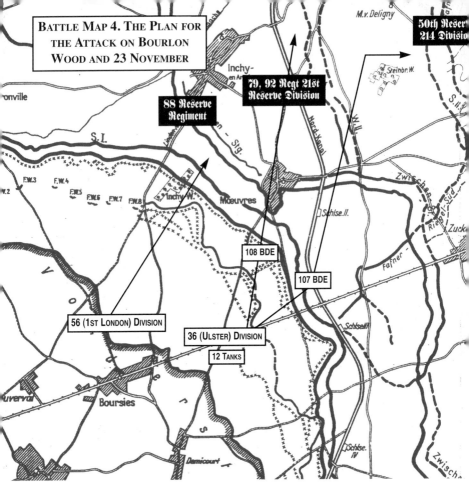

BATTLE MAP 4. THE PLAN FOR THE ATTACK ON BOURLON WOOD AND 23 NOVEMBER

50th Reser 214 Divisio

M.v. Deligny

Steinbr. W.

79, 92 Regt 21st Reserve Division

88 Reserve Regiment

Inchy-en-Ar

onville

S.I.

108 BDE

107 BDE

F.W.3 F.W.4

F.W.5 F.W.6 F.W.7 F.W.8

Inchy W. Mœuvres

Schlse. II.

56 (1ST LONDON) DIVISION

36 (ULSTER) DIVISION

12 TANKS

Schlse II.

uverval Boursies

Damicourt

Schlse. IV

give them time to prepare, after 20 November they had rallied at Ribécourt and in Havrincourt Wood, where repairs, maintenance, resupplying with fuel and ammunition took place. Vitally, new crew members were provided, replacing those who could no longer carry on. Zero hour for the whole attack would be 10.30am, with the artillery barrage commencing only twenty minutes earlier to coincide with the advance of the tanks, emulating the initial, stunning tactic of the first day.

The Attack on the Right flank

What of the German opposition? Fontaine was defended by the II/46th Regiment, part of the II/50th Regiment, and the machine gun company of the III/46th. Between Bourlon and La Folie Wood were troops of General Havenstein's 107th Division: during the day the 58th

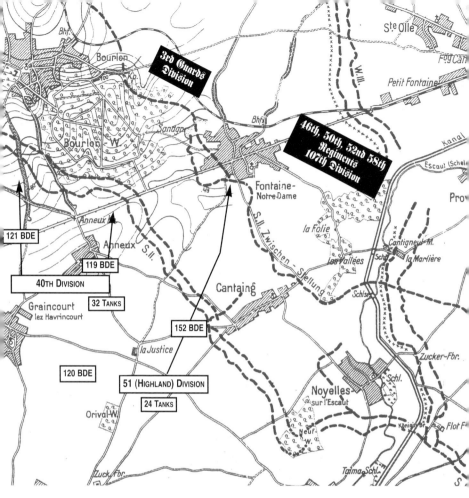

and the 52nd Regiments from the 107th Division arrived. In the wood was the 3rd Guards Division, a most formidable force which outnumbered Major General Harper's Highlanders, who had been in action now since dawn on the 20th and whose right flank was completely open. Further, the Germans had got over the shock of the first day and the tank now held fewer terrors for them.

23rd November 6.30am.

It was a cold, wet and windy morning and dawn had not yet broken. Although the attack was not scheduled to start until 10.30am, Brigadier Burn (commanding 152 Brigade, consisting of 1/6th Gordons, 1/6th Seaforths, 1/8th Argylls and the 1/5th Seaforths) moved the first two battalions into position in the sunken Premy Chapel-Graincourt Road. They would carry out the attack, supported

235th Brigade (47th Divisional Artillery) watering horses in Flesquières, 24 November 1917.

by the Argylls who were sheltering in Orival Wood until required and the 1/5th Seaforths, who were in reserve in Flesquières. On the right flank Lieutenant Colonel the Hon W. Fraser would take his 1/6th Gordons to the southern edge of Fontaine with twelve tanks. On his right, less than 800 yards away, was the strongly held and bunkered La Folie Wood, part of the Hindenburg Switch Line. Colonel Fraser, appreciating the danger posed by the wood, asked for a smoke barrage to obscure his advance; however the artillery had none, finding it hard enough to get itself and sufficient high explosive shells up to a suitable position as it was. This would prove crucial. At 10.10am the barrage fell on a line in front of Fontaine and twenty minutes later lifted for 200 yards; at that the twelve tanks allotted to the Gordons moved forward, as did the infantry. Two other circumstances now occurred to frustrate Colonel Fraser, one of them really General Harper's fault. First, eleven of the tanks were female, and though they dispersed many groups of the 1st Battalion, 46th Reserve Regiment, they could not eliminate or silence the machine gun fire coming from the Chateau bunkers. The male tank, with its six-pounders, was knocked out at the very start. The other problem was the reluctance of the infantry to keep up with the tanks. One might have thought that their experience at Flesquières would have taught them the importance of doing this. Perhaps it would not have made much difference, for the tremendous machine gun fire

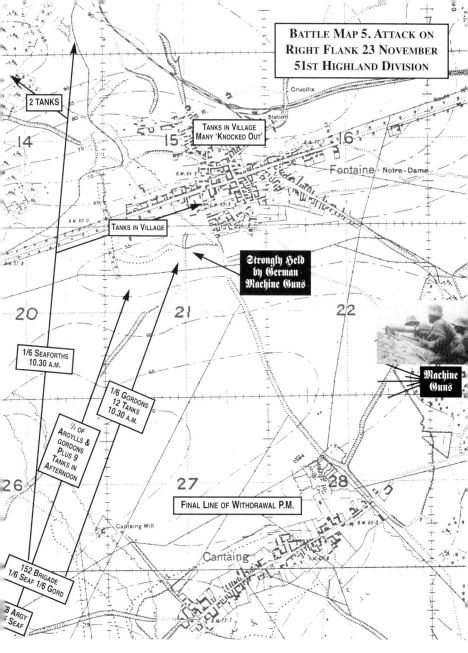

BATTLE MAP 5. ATTACK ON
RIGHT FLANK 23 NOVEMBER
51ST HIGHLAND DIVISION

2 TANKS

Crucifix

Station

14

15

TANKS IN VILLAGE
MANY 'KNOCKED OUT'

16

Fontaine - Notre - Dame

B.M. 64 9

B.M. 62 0

TANKS IN VILLAGE

B.M. 57 9

Strongly Held
by German
Machine Guns

20

21

22

Machine
Guns

1/6 SEAFORTHS
10.30 A.M.

1/6 GORDONS
12 TANKS
10.30 A.M.

½ OF
ARGYLLS &
GORDONS
PLUS 9
TANKS IN
AFTERNOON

26

27

28

FINAL LINE OF WITHDRAWAL P.M.

Cantaing Mill

B.M. 60 3

152 BRIGADE
1/6 SEAF 1/6 GORD

Cantaing

8 ARGY
SEAF

B.M. 12 7

brought the Gordons to a halt some 500 yards short of the village, where they dug in. The tanks were also having a hard time, for although the Mark IV was proof against armour piercing ammunition, it was not against the sheer volume of it. Nevertheless they continued

47

Ruins of the main chateau at the north west end of Bourlon. A. Boyer

into Fontaine but at the end of the day only three returned to their base. Brigadier General Burn brought up the 1/5th Seaforths in the afternoon, two companies of Argylls, a hundred men of the 1/6th Gordons and nine more tanks. He hoped to bomb into Fontaine from the west but the deep sunken road to the south of Fontaine housed many Germans in deep dugouts and the attack was repulsed, with the loss of two more tanks.

On the left of the Brigade's attack the 1/6th Seaforths with fifteen tanks had also set out on the same time scale that morning. The task was to clear the eastern slope of Bourlon between Fontaine and to link up with the Gordons on the right but that did not take place. The initial advance went well; some of the tanks went into the western end of the village whilst the Seaforths were tackling the German infantry and machine gunners. They reached the north-eastern extremity of the wood, about 1,000 yards north of the main Bapaume - Cambrai road and close to the railway line. Two of the tanks went into the wood and fought there all day with the 40th Division, but only one returned. German counter attacks which came from over the shoulder of the hill were stopped by tanks and infantry, but by evening - and because of the failure on the right flank - the Seaforths could make no entry into Fontaine. They did establish a line of posts from the entrance to the wood at the Bourlon-Fontaine road down to Cantaing. The tank crews had fought bravely. Forty-eight had been involved overall, but those who had gone into the village had done so without infantry support. A great many were holed and damaged and a dozen were immobilised and left behind. The casualties amongst the twelve crews that advanced with the Seaforths were nine officers and twenty other ranks alone. Captain Hotblack, one of Brigadier General Elles's original Staff, won a Bar to his DSO for his example and initiative in helping the infantry and collecting the tanks whilst under a murderous barrage and machine

A Mark IV tank (C44) captured by the Germans, ditched near La Vacquerie.

gun fire. By nightfall on the 23rd the attack on the right flank had come to an end and once again the hoped for Cavalry advance had been denied. The 1st Cavalry Division did not retire from the area but remained at Graincourt at the disposal of the 40th Division. With two brigades in reserve it is difficult to understand why General Harper did not force the capture of Fontaine. His men were tired, but with the number of tanks at his disposal it would seem quite feasible that the village could have been both taken and retained.

The Attack in The Centre: 23rd November, 6.30am

40th Division's orders for the 23rd were simple: capture Bourlon Wood and the village and then form a defensive line running east to west, north of the village and with its right on the railway cutting. On the right was the 51st Division and on the left the 36th. The right Brigade, 119 (Brigadier General F.P. Crozier) with sixteen tanks, would clear Bourlon Wood, a front of 1,500 yards and perhaps 2,000 deep. The left brigade, 121 (Brigadier General J. Campbell) with thirteen tanks would capture the western shoulder of Bourlon Ridge and the village itself, a battle line width of 2,000 yards and an advance of 3,000 yards. The infantry had never seen tanks before and there was

Senior officer visiting German troops near Bourlon. A. Boyer

no time to train them. However, sheer initiative and determination, with the simple instruction, 'keep close but not too close, follow them through the wire', was enough. Observers said later: The Welshmen charged magnificently into the trees. 120 Brigade (Brigadier General Willoughby) was in reserve at Havrincourt. Both 119 and 121 Brigades would mount their attacks simultaneously, their joint boundary being the western edge of the wood. Ahead of them were the German defenders, the 50th Regiment of the 214th Division in the village and the wood whilst the Lehr Regiment of the 3rd Guards Division was in the process of arriving in the wood. More troops would soon be on their way but insufficient were there to mount a full scale counter attack for three more days.

Before dawn the battalions started to get themselves in position. The 62nd Division's earlier battle was much in evidence, wrecked trenches and barbed wire strewn with many dead - there had been no time to move them. The Welshmen of 119 Brigade, in and about the sunken road and Anneux, were cold, wet and tired whilst their thoughts as they looked up into the dense, wet, mass of trees on the hill rising in front of them can only be imagined. No one in the Division had any idea of the ground ahead, they had never seen it. In fact the layout of the wood was not unlike an English one, with rides leading across it and into the village.

On the right of 119 Brigade was Lieutenant Colonel Plunkett's 19th Royal Welch Fusiliers. On the left was the 12th South Wales Borderers (Lieutenant Colonel R. Benzie) which had all of the twelve tanks allotted to the attack; and on the flanks of the Brigade was the 17th Welch Regiment.

At daybreak all was quiet, but the silence was disturbed by flights of British planes. Fifty fighters had been allotted to support the infantry, swooping over to shoot into the trees as the hours to Zero ticked by. There was much enemy air activity also, amongst others

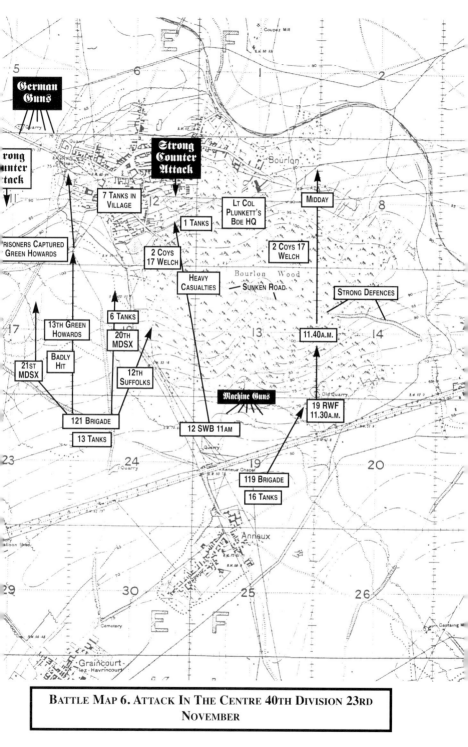

German Guns

Strong Counter Attack

Strong Counter Attack

Bourlon

7 Tanks in Village

1 Tanks

Lt Col Plunkett's Bde HQ

Midday

Prisoners Captured Green Howards

2 Coys 17 Welch

2 Coys 17 Welch

Heavy Casualties

Bourlon Wood

Sunken Road

Strong Defences

13th Green Howards

6 Tanks

20th MDSX

Badly Hit

21st MDSX

12th Suffolks

11.40 A.M.

121 Brigade

13 Tanks

Machine Guns

12 SWB 11AM

19 RWF 11.30 A.M.

119 Brigade

16 Tanks

Anneux

Graincourt-lez-Havrincourt

BATTLE MAP 6. ATTACK IN THE CENTRE 40TH DIVISION 23RD NOVEMBER

Manfred von Richthofen's aircraft were here. During the day Lieutenant J.A.V. Boddy, of 64 Squadron, flying a DH5, was wounded in the head and crashed in the south-east corner of the wood, fortunately to be rescued by another crashed pilot. Tanks now came up from the south and the 158 guns, including two 6" howitzer batteries and two 60-pounder batteries would soon begin their barrage. Unfortunately, as had happened on the right with the 51st Division, they had not brought smoke; some of the infantry had a 1000 yards of open ground to cross and then mount a slope to get into the wood. At 10.10am the barrage began, at 10.30am the first lift of 200 yards took place (to be followed by further jumps every ten minutes) and the infantry began their march into the unknown. The attack orders were that the tanks would pass through the infantry at 10.50am and advance, the infantry following 100 to 200 yards behind them, all preceded by the artillery barrage. The shelling was by no means all one way, for the German guns had been shooting since about 8am and Major H.P. Coles of the 19th Royal Welch Fusiliers had been knocked out by their shellfire at 9am. On time, just before 11am, the Fusiliers were the first of 119 Brigade to get into the wood, pushing through the enemy barrage regardless of casualties. Machine gun fire from the wood was slight; after crossing an enemy trench on the southern face and entering into the undergrowth, the Battalion stopped at the quarry to reorganise before continuing. Ahead of them was a 1 in 20 climb through the trees. After about 800 yards the partly sunken track from Fontaine was reached; this crossed the top of the spur (about a hundred feet high), and was intersected by tracks going north until it entered the south-east corner of Bourlon village. On the left the 12th South Wales Borderers advanced on a line slightly south-west of the Fusiliers. They got off well but were soon met by heavy machine gun fire coming from a sunken track zig-zagging across the lower slope. The Borderers went for these guns with the bayonet. Private Plummer, driving forward alone, cleared a strong point to take eight prisoners and then repeated his fierce attack, capturing a machine gun and a further sixteen prisoners. He survived the battle and was awarded the DCM; but casualties in his Battalion were becoming heavy. Both battalions were now amongst the German main resistance line where in the clearings the Germans had established strong points with good fields of fire. The din of battle was frightening as the German shells crashed amongst the trees bringing them down onto the Welshmen. The few tanks had great difficulties in moving forward, endeavouring to thread their way forward through the disintegrating forest. They proved their worth as

Bourlon, the main street. The railway station is to the right, and the wood is beyond the houses on the left. The church is in the background. A. Boyer

from time to time they were invaluable in overcoming specific defence sites. By 11.40am both battalions had got into the strongly defended Fontaine to Bourlon track. They halted there briefly to reorganise, an essential stop in the almost impossible going; at this stage both of them had suffered at least 100 casualties, but they now pressed on across the top of the hill. The situation at midday was hopeful. On the right Plunkett's Fusiliers had emerged from the northern edge of the wood and he went forward to organise a front defence line round the top of the descending slope, going round the eastern corner of the wood. They could see what appeared to be bodies of the enemy retiring to the north-east. Lieutenant Colonel Benzie's South Wales men were in a more difficult situation on the left. They too had reached the northern edge, but owing to high casualties were somewhat disorganised. At 1pm, Major Brown went forward to regroup the line and found that at least fifteen of the officers who had started out were now casualties. As he arrived so began the first German counter attack, which pushed the right flank of the Battalion back to the sunken road. However a tank appeared and with it a stand was made, enabling Captain Symes with his platoon to extricate themselves from being cut off in the village. Both battalions now occupied some of the houses on the edge of the village. At this stage the 17th Welch Regiment became involved in the fight and the 18th Welch were brought out of reserve at Anneux and entered the battle. Bourlon Hill was busy with Welshmen. The afternoon would bring great pressure from the Germans along the whole front of the hill; but reinforcements of dismounted cavalry and men from 120 Brigade would arrive to assist Lieutenant Colonel Plunkett, who had been given command of the whole of 119 Brigade's line. He put his HQ into a red bricked chalet just north of the centre of the wood and a number of tracks to Bourlon. Near this he dug his main defence on the 100 metre contour line. Lieutenant Colonel Benzie of the 12th South Wales Borderers was placed in command of the forward area.

23rd November 6.30am: Left flank of the 40th Division.

Brigadier General J. Campbell received the Divisional attack orders shortly after midnight. At 3am he met his Battalion and Machine Gun Company commanders in the ruined Sugar Factory on the main road, north of Graincourt. After explaining the operation he issued verbal orders:

> *The 20th Middlesex is to be on the right, their nearest neighbours the 12th South Wales Borderers. The Battalion's objective, the Spur protruding from Bourlon Wood, just below the village. The 13th Yorkshires,* [Green Howards] *who would advance on the left of the Middlesex in conjunction with the 107th Brigade of the 36th Division on their left. Later the Yorkshiremen will pivot right on the Middlesex and attack Bourlon from the west whilst the Middlesex will thrust at it from the south with Brigadier General Crozier's 119th Brigade coming up through the Wood. The 21st Middlesex will move in support of the 13th Yorkshires to their left rear, covering its flanks in the event of 107 Brigade being held up. The Reserve Battalion, the 12th Suffolks, will wait in the trenches south of the main road near Graincourt. The Machine Gun Company will open up a barrage from the Sugar Factory covering the left flank. Six tanks will lead the Middlesex; in total it is hoped that twelve will be available.*

At dawn the German artillery began its attack on the Brigade. The Green Howards suffered heavily from guns firing from Quarry Wood, 3000 yards to the north-west; Second Lieutenant Stanford was killed almost immediately. As elsewhere on the Division's front, at 10.30am the infantry began its advance across the treeless and gradually rising slope, slashed with a number of sunken roads, German trenches and barbed wire. It had snowed during the night and now there was incessant rain; almost at the start things began to go wrong. The 36th Division came up against the fresh 21st Reserve Division, the 79th Regiment and the II/92nd Regiment, part of the 20th Division, and was held up, particularly 107 Brigade. Without their support the Green Howards were forced inwards; Captain Mason, Lieutenants Walton, Phillips and June were killed, with several other officers wounded and about fifty other rank casualties. However the attack to the north behind the tanks kept going and at midday the Middlesex had crossed the Spur, their objective, and some were seen entering the southern corner of the village. The Green Howards had captured sixty prisoners near the crucifix, half a mile west of Bourlon, but a German counter attack freed them. The 21st Middlesex went forward into the left flank but could get no further; of the six tanks leading the 20th Middlesex, three received direct hits. In the end seven tanks entered the village, of which three had to retire. The whole advance was swept with shell and machine gun fire, and there was never any prospect of Brigadier Campbell's Brigade driving the enemy out of the village. German resistance was increasing and their artillery fired unceasingly. The Yorkshires had been ejected from a house near the Chateau on the north west corner. The early good news from 107 Brigade of its advance was soon shattered. By early evening 121 Brigade's operation for the day was finished, its units strung out from Bourlon village southwards to the Bapaume - Cambrai road. Brigadier General Campbell was told, 'The Green Howards and the 21st Middlesex practically obliterated'. The 12th Suffolks were on the right of the line

German machine gun team poised for action.

in touch with the Welshmen whilst all the battalions of 121 Brigade were considerably intermingled. The casualties were severe and there had been many fine examples of individual heroism. For example, CSM Edward Hall, of the 21st Middlesex, took command of his Company when the OC was killed although he himself was wounded three times, and remained at his post.

Brigadier Crozier's 119 Brigade had also come to a halt by the evening. At 3.10pm a German counter attack behind a barrage of 5.9s, 4.2s and 77s had come through the village and forced the left back to the central cross ride; but the 18th Welch had managed to recover some of their line. In doing so Lieutenant Colonel Kennedy was killed by a bullet while leading them forward,

> *One of the finest commanders a battalion could wish for, who*
> *rode right up to us on his horse, jumped off and rushing in front*
> *of us rallied us, waving his cane urging us·on, going only a few*
> *yards before he was slain.*

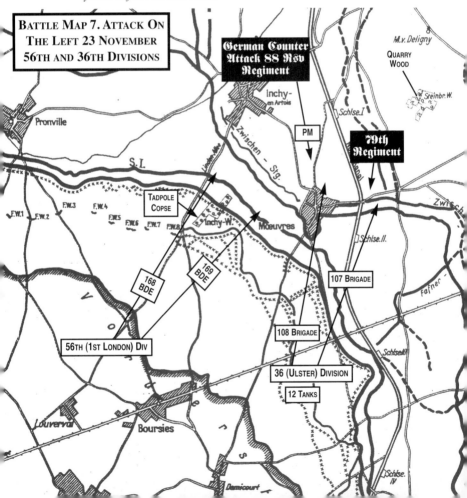

BATTLE MAP 7. ATTACK ON THE LEFT 23 NOVEMBER 56TH AND 36TH DIVISIONS

His second-in-command was also wounded and command of the Battalion was taken over by the Adjutant, Captain F.H. Mathias. It was at this critical time that CSM Davies of the 18th, who was leading his company when the commander fell wounded, actually rushed forward in the open to kneel down so that his shoulder could be used to support the firing of a Lewis gun until he collapsed from a wound in the head. Such was the ferocity of the Welshmen's attack. Bourlon Wood and village had not yet been taken but misleading information, mainly from Royal Flying Corps observation, that the British held Fontaine and Bourlon villages had been sent to IV Corps HQ. There was a scene from hell in the wood: the constant crashing of shells bringing down trees, the visibility almost zero with groups of friends and foes bumping into one another, with vicious hand to hand fighting. German snipers seemed to fire from all points of the compass; whilst there was no coherent defensive front. There was a now obvious increase in German strength and their repeated attacks in the dark night might have been too much for lesser men; but not for those Welsh of Brigadier General Crozier's Brigade. Crozier was personally a brave man; he believed that he had to hold a position regardless of casualties until ordered to withdraw. It is recorded that he approved of men being shot by their own if they failed to stand with their comrades. 119 Brigade would stand, succeed or die here but would never withdraw without orders.

German troops assemble for a night attack.

German dead in Bourlon Wood. P. Gorczynski

During the night of the 23rd, various measures were taken which were designed to enable the capture of the wood and village on the 24th; that attack would begin at 3pm. Although Brigadier General Willoughby's 120 Brigade was not here as a formation, almost all of its composite battalions would be. The remaining two companies of Lieutenant Colonel J. Couper's 14th Argylls and the dismounted 15th Hussars (part of the 9th Cavalry Battalion) along with eight machine guns from 204th Machine Gun Company came up to Lieutenant

Colonel Plunkett. Lieutenant Colonel Battye's 14th Highland Light Infantry with twelve tanks would attack the village with Lieutenant Colonel H.L.Warden's 13th East Surreys, passing through 121 Brigade. They would be accompanied by companies from the dismounted 9th Cavalry Battalion, provided by the 19th Hussars and the 1st Bedfordfordshire Yeomanry, all of which were placed under Brigadier General Campbell's orders; they took over the left of 121 Brigade. The 13th Green Howards and the 21st Middlesex had indeed been severely hurt and that night were withdrawn into reserve at Graincourt.

On the far left of the attack that morning the 56th Division had extended its hold on the Hindenburg Line front system beyond Tadpole Copse. The 36th Division, despite being most successful in its assault on Moeuvres and capturing three-quarters of the village and its defence system, was forced to relinquish its hold. It retired to the southern edge of the village after a German counter attack from the direction of Inchy by the II/88th Reserve Regiment of the 21st Reserve Division.

At 8pm that night the Commander-in-Chief, concerned that the chance of securing and holding the Bourlon Ridge should not be missed through lack of troops, told General Byng that dismounted cavalry in 'any numbers' should be used if required.

In the meantime Major General G.P.T. Feilding's Guards Division had been brought up from Bapaume. It was hoped that after the capture of Fontaine by the 51st (Highland) Division and Bourlon by the 40th on the 23rd, General Feilding's men would break out to the north. Unaware of the developing situation, General Feilding proceeded to make a reconnaissance of the country. In his absence, and because of the situation existing at the end of the 23rd, his Division was ordered to relieve the 51st Highland Division at Fontaine that night. Despite the short notice, distance and the difficulties in finding the various headquarters of the 51st because of the very poor communications and awful weather, Brigadier General C.R. Champion de Crespigny's 1 Guards Brigade had by midnight taken over the front at Fontaine. The 3 Guards Brigade (Brigadier General Lord Henry Seymour) was in support at Flesquières.

The 51st (Highland) Division had suffered casualties totalling 68 officers and 1,502 other ranks in the period 20th-23rd November.

24th November (Saturday)

Other reinforcements besides the Guards were also in sight; the two divisions whose transfer to Italy had been cancelled were on their way. Major General C.E. Pereira's 2nd Division, 5, 6 and 99 Brigades came down from Flanders by rail and Major General Sir G.F. Gorringe's 47th (2/London) Division, 140,141 and 142 Brigades, was arriving west of Bapaume in the area of the two Achiets. IV Corps ordered the 40th Division to be relieved on the night of 25/26 November by the 62nd (2/West Riding) Division, 185,186 and 187 Brigades, which had itself only been relieved on the night of the 22/23rd after suffering 1,698 casualties. Much later in the night, after a particularly busy day, the 2nd Scots Guards of 3 Guards Brigade from La Justice, with two companies of the 11th Kings Own from 120 Brigade, arrived to fill a gap on the right of 119 Brigade's line. This provided a link with 1 Guards Brigade. The main aim on this day of high winds and heavy rain was to be centred on Bourlon. On the extreme left the 56th Division was to secure the Hindenburg System north of Tadpole Copse whilst the 36th Division would maintain its hold on the Canal Du Nord at Lock 5, a mile south east of Moeuvres. In the event the Ulster men stayed where they were but the 56th Division were driven back along the Hindenburg Support System. Its day had been singularly unsuccessful.

In Bourlon Wood and village were the Lehr Regiment of the 3rd Guards Division and in the German east to west line the 9th Grenadiers with some of the I/175th Regiment and the III/88th Reserve Regiment. In reserve was the Guards Fusilier Regiment. This provided a strong force to carry out the German counter-attack which would, at 8pm, be reinforced by the 46th Reserve Regiment of the 49th Division. The 221st Division was also about to arrive. By any standards it was going to be a difficult day for the scattered and exhausted men of the two front line commanders in the wood, Lieutenant Colonels Benzie and Plunkett.

During the night a warning order was received to prepare for the renewal of the attack on Bourlon village. Because the 14th Argylls had already been sucked into 119 Brigade in the wood, the attack would be made by Lieutenant Colonel Battye's 14th Highland Light Infantry on the right and Lieutenant Colonel Eardley Wilmot's 12th Suffolks on the left. There would be twelve tanks.

This was to be the day's main event. Brigadier Crozier's 119 Brigade would complete the capture of the wood. Certainly the capture of the village without the wood would not be possible.

Brigadier General Campbell was told verbally that Zero hour for the village battle would be at 3pm on the 24th, the tanks advancing at 3.20pm. The initial attack would be in three stages, the first objective

The main square in Bourlon, looking east. A. Boyer

the outer edge, the second the inner edge and the third the northern outskirts. On each objective there would be a 'mopping up' halt of twenty minutes, which was especially stressed by the General, wise to the Germans' practice of sheltering in the houses to fire into the backs of the attackers. Once they had entered the village the tanks would remain at the important cross roads and form strong points. The British heavy bombardment would be from Zero minus one hour to twenty minutes afterwards, lifting to the north side of the village. It would also form a defensive wall when the advance was secured. Although Campbell had been given all this verbally he had not received definite instructions.

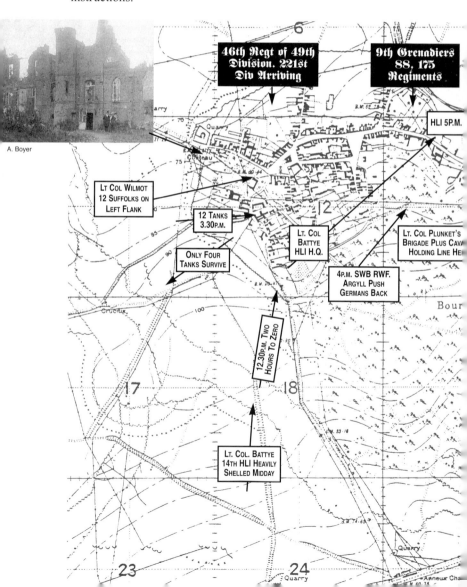

A. Boyer

46th Regt of 49th Division. 221st Div Arriving

9th Grenadiers 88, 175 Regiments

HLI 5P.M.

Lt Col Wilmot 12 Suffolks on Left Flank

12 Tanks 3.30P.M.

Only Four Tanks Survive

Lt. Col Battye HLI H.Q.

Lt. Col Plunket's Brigade Plus Cav Holding Line He

4P.M. SWB RWF. Argyll Push Germans Back

Bour

12.30P.M. Two Hours To Zero

Lt. Col. Battye 14th HLI Heavily Shelled Midday

Quarry

Anneux Cha

During the morning the Corps Commander (with General Ponsonby) decided that because only twelve tanks were available the attack should be postponed until there were more. Because of the extreme difficulty of communications – the perennial problem of the Great War - Campbell did not receive the new orders. Consequently he confirmed what he understood to be the plan and timings to the attacking force. The attack would go ahead.

The morning was one of extreme pressure in the wood, with the Germans making heavy attacks on 119 Brigade and its increased support.

The 14th HLI began to move forward from Graincourt at midday

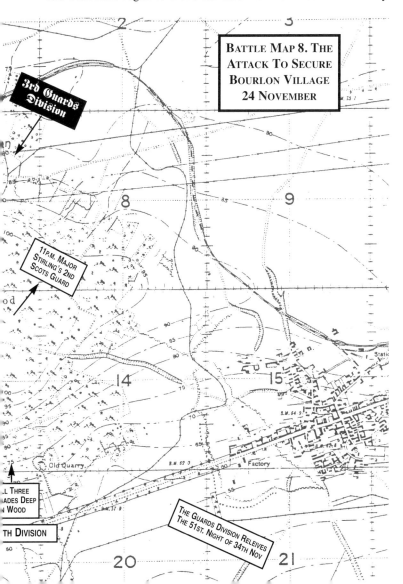

BATTLE MAP 8. THE ATTACK TO SECURE BOURLON VILLAGE 24 NOVEMBER

and were instantly seen by the Germans on the ridge, who began to shell the Battalion out in the open, blasting No. 7 Platoon, wiping it out except for its Lieutenant and his batman. The rest of the Scotsmen just plodded stoically forward through the barrage, arriving at the rendezvous in the Wood on the edge of the village at 12.30pm; they had two and a half hours to wait.

In fact two separate battles would, effectively, be fought: one in the wood and the other in the village. The Germans fully understood that control of the hill was of paramount importance; if it fell the village would fall. Unaware of the imminent attack on the village, at 3pm they attacked in force, coming up the slope from the east and north-east. This narrative will be told later.

At 3.30pm the twelve tanks entered the village. There were some hundreds of the enemy hiding in the cellars and using the loopholed walls of the houses as forts. They were not surprised to see the tanks advancing without supporting infantry and within a short span of time the tanks were compelled to withdraw. Five had broken down, one had its petrol tank pierced and was abandoned, one got stuck in a deep ditch and an eighth received a direct hit and burnt out. Those of the crews who had survived managing to get on board the remaining four as they retired from the village; once again they had not seen any British infantry.

The HLI, leading the infantry advance, came along the southern edge of the village, amongst the trees, their objective being the north-east corner where the railway curved into the village and then went north through a cutting. Sheltered as they were, little opposition was met and at 4pm their companies reported arriving at the German trenches beyond the village's north-eastern corner. Prisoners had been

Bourlon village as it looked in 1918.

taken and Lieutenant Colonel Battye put his HQ and fourth company in a farmhouse 500 yards south-east of the church. There was a large gap between him and the other three companies across the village at the railway. At 5pm he informed Brigade HQ of the progress, and that his casualties were very light, a mere thirty five men.

The 12th Suffolks advanced behind, to the left and north of the Scotsmen. They came under attack as soon as they advanced, with heavy machine gun fire sweeping into their left flank from the German trenches in the Marquion Line, a 1000 yards to the north-west, and from the houses in the village beyond the Chateau and the village church. Strong local counter attacks by the Lehr Battalion drove them back. 119 Brigade was under attack in the wood, so that at 5pm the 14th HLI were isolated at the far end of the village. It was now dark and the Glaswegians could hear the Germans shouting orders; they were in amongst some hundreds of the enemy.

As soon as Major General Ponsonby was aware that the Brigade attack on the village had begun he ordered all that was left of 120 Brigade into Brigadier General Campbell's command, that is the 13th East Surreys, the King's Own and the Brigade's Machine Gun Company.

Men were shot from unexpected quarters, runners sent out to contact Battalion HQ never arrived and company commanders struggled to form defensive positions without knowing the precise locations of the enemy, although it was obvious that they were surrounded. The three leading companies were in and about the railway station and the junction on the northern edge whilst the fourth company and Battalion HQ were cut off from them, somewhere south of the main east to west street, which was occupied by the enemy.

Whilst all this was going on the Germans were maintaining pressure on Lieutenant Colonel Plunkett's command on the northern part of the hill by firing incessant high explosive and gas shells. His HQ in the red bricked chalet was now a total ruin and a deadly place to be. At 3pm the enemy attack succeeded in driving 119 Brigade back for 300 yards to the sunken road, the track from Fontaine to Bourlon, the centre line of the wood. However Brigadier General Crozier's men, exhausted as they were, would not give in. With an almost super human effort the South Wales Borderers, the Royal Welch Fusiliers, the Argylls and the dismounted Hussars fought to push the Germans back across the hill top to the northern slope of the wood, allowing the 17th Welch Regiment to fight their way out. At about 9.30pm the 2nd Scots Guards, led by Major Jack Stirling, arrived at the sunken road leading north from Anneux Chapel. Lieutenant Colonel Benzie told them to deploy on the right flank, linking up with 1 Guards Brigade at Fontaine. However Benzie knew little of the situation deep in the wood and Major Stirling, moving his men forward through the trees, found Lieutenant Colonel Plunkett at a point south of the main cross ride at about 11pm. The German machine gun barrages were almost unceasing, firing down the north to south ride which effectively bisects the wood. Plunkett asked Stirling to occupy the high ground, hoping that he could get in touch with troops in Bourlon village. He was not aware of the situation there. Lieutenant Colonel Plunkett had only one surviving senior officer to help him control the remnants of his five battalion command; and he was wounded as Stirling arrived. To find out what was in front of him in the village Major Stirling sent out a patrol under Second Lieutenant J.R. Hamilton. It was destroyed, though Hamilton survived his wounds. More Scots Guards were sent out and discovered that Bourlon was in German, not British, possession. The Battalion now took up a line with its right on the eastern margin, extending north westwards for about a 1000 yards. Stirling also found the wood was alive with Germans. Three hundred yards north of him, approximately in the centre of the wood and at a cross roads, was a strongly held strong point equipped with several machine guns. The Scots Guards settled in after a good deal of close quarter fighting and waited for daylight. That night the highest part of the hill was once again in British hands.

Already plans were being made by General Byng to attack the village again on the following day, the 25th. Extensive use of the Cavalry Corps would be made to exploit north of Bourlon, whilst the 40th Division, despite its exhausted state, assisted by many tanks would capture Bourlon. In fact no tanks could be had, as they had all been withdrawn for refitting. Such was the difficulty with communications in this far ranging battle.

The day drew to a close with a Special Order of The Day from the Commander-in-Chief, thanking Commanders and all ranks of all arms and services for their exertions and congratulating them on the success so far achieved,

> *The capture of the important Bourlon position yesterday crowns a most successful operation and opens the way to a further exploitation of the advantage already gained.*

The Special Order was at the least premature, showing clearly Sir Douglas Haig's anxiety. On the 25th he recommended General Byng to assume personal control.

Finally, on the 24th, Crown Prince Rupprecht was told that a counter attack could be launched on the 27th, as sufficient artillery ammunition would have arrived; but he was content for the next two days to allow the British to continue their efforts in the north, thereby dissipating their strength.

25th of November

It had been a stormy night but day brought a bright sky, allowing for good observation. During the small hours preparations were made to go into Bourlon, to join up with the 14th HLI The confusion and intermingling of units was considerable. On the western side the forward positions connecting on the left with the 36th Division were only a line of posts, some impossible to approach in daylight. These were held by the 12th Suffolks and men from two dismounted battalions (1st and 9th) of the 1st Cavalry Division, the 2nd and 5th Dragoon Guards and the 11th Hussars under Major Rome. Three thousand yards south, on the Cambrai road, about the factory were grouped the survivors of the 13th Yorkshires (only four officers and 120 men) and the 20th and 21st Middlesex. The only fresh troops at hand were the 13th East Surreys and two companies of the 11th King's Own. Only one battalion would advance into Bourlon, the East Surreys, and they would go without either tanks and artillery support because the village could not be shelled owing to the presence of the14th HLI. The East Surreys were unaware that there would be no tanks.

At 2pm Divisional HQ issued orders for the attack with tanks. It had no knowledge of the situation in the village, nor that there would be no tanks. Lieutenant Colonel Warden, commanding the Surreys, was ordered to clear the western part of the village with these non-existent machines. He started from Graincourt in the late evening of the 24th to meet Lieutenant Colonel Battye in the wood, and sent back a message for his Battalion to meet him in the Quarry, half a mile west of Anneux Chapel, at 3.30am. He was told at Battye's HQ that there were no British troops north of the cross roads just beyond the Quarry and that the Glasgow battalion had been wiped out. Undeterred, he pushed on into the wood under the German barrage falling on the south-west part of the wood. He believed that the shelling was designed to stop reinforcements reaching the HLI Accordingly he decided to bring up his Battalion in the dark, intercepting it on its march north of Graincourt, and led them to the sunken road going north on the edge of the wood which was under bombardment with gas shells at this time. Warden halted his men to explain the scheme for capturing the village. At 6am he stopped just south of the village. His plan was that the leading platoon of each company would go straight through the village whilst it was still dark and join the HLI at the railway station. The remainder would mop up the Germans in the village proper whilst the fourth company would be in reserve at the north west corner of the Wood, shielded by trees. Zero hour would be 6.15am. He was still expecting a dozen tanks but, of course, at Zero none had arrived. Undeterred, he gave the order to advance and he reached the 14th HLI HQ a few hundred yards south east of the church. With him he had a written message for Lieutenant Colonel Battye from Brigadier General

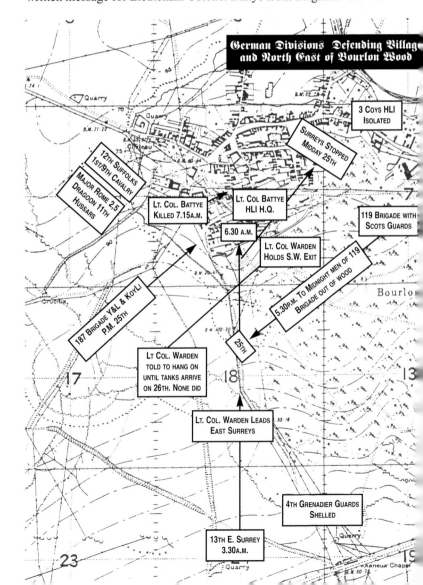

German Divisions Defending Village and North East of Bourlon Wood

Quarry

Quarry

3 Coys HLI Isolated

Surreys Stopped Midday 25th

12th Suffolks 1st/9th Cavalry

Major Rome 2.5 Dragoon 11th Hussars

Lt. Col. Battye Killed 7.15a.m.

Lt. Col Battye HLI H.Q.

119 Brigade with Scots Guards

6.30 a.m.

Lt. Col Warden Holds S.W. Exit

5.30p.m. To Midnight men of 119 Brigade out of wood

Bourlo

Crucifix

187 Brigade Y&L & KoYLI P.M. 25th

25th

Lt Col. Warden told to hang on until tanks arrive on 26th. None did

Lt. Col. Warden Leads East Surreys

4th Grenadier Guards Shelled

Quarry

13th E. Surrey 3.30a.m.

Quarry

Anneux Chapel

Campbell. As the two commanding officers spoke together, intense fire swept into the house from all sides. The attack on the building was repelled by the HLI reserve company and some of the East Surreys. All the men in the two battalions were heavily involved in fighting in the village streets. At 7.15am Battye left the house, crossing the road behind to visit a Lewis gun position, when a burst of machine gun fire swept down the road, hitting him in the heart. He staggered back to the house to tell Warden he had been hit and collapsed and died. Lieutenant Colonel Warden was now in command. He now read the message from the Brigadier General, timed at 5.20am, which said that the HLI were to capture (with tanks) the re-entrant at the railway

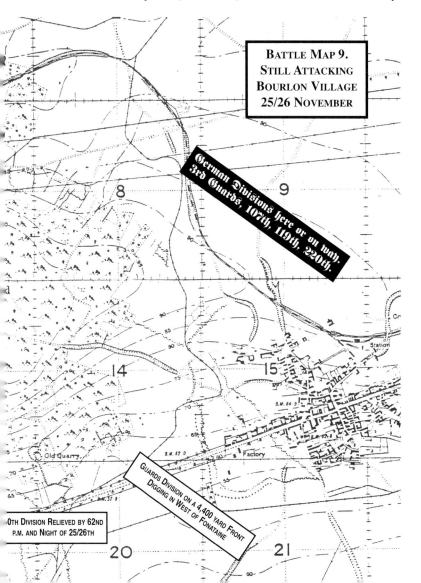

BATTLE MAP 9.
STILL ATTACKING
BOURLON VILLAGE
25/26 NOVEMBER

German Divisions here or on way.
3rd Guards, 107th, 119th, 220th.

GUARDS DIVISION ON A 4,400 YARD FRONT
DIGGING IN WEST OF FONATAINE

0TH DIVISION RELIEVED BY 62ND
P.M. AND NIGHT OF 25/26TH

station to allow the cavalry through. The attack was to be at 9am. It was impossible to comply with the message. Further, no contact had been made with 119 Brigade, somewhere behind him in the wood, as visibility at 7.45am was very difficult through the undergrowth and in the early light. He decided to try and make contact with the Brigade, but this was forestalled by a large force of Germans advancing from the east. The attack was driven off. What he did not know then was that the HLI at the station had been compelled to surrender at about 9.30am; of the three companies there, there were only eighty survivors. The total casualties to the 14th HLI in the fighting at Bourlon amounted to 17 officers and 426 other ranks. It was a sad ending for a brave battalion. Their Colonel was buried in the garden of the house where he had died.

The East Surreys could make no progress through the village to help the HLI at the railway station in the face of powerful German opposition, who by now were attacking almost all of the buildings. One company set about converting the combined Battalions' HQ into a redoubt, repelling attacks from the north, east and south. By mid-morning the two companies in the village began to drift back and Warden's HQ became a bastion on the left front of 119 Brigade, securing the exit from the village on the south-western corner. As the day wore on, the fighting never ending, contact was made with 119 Brigade; the Brigade itself was attacked once again at about noon, but Lieutenant Colonel Plunkett's counter with two companies of Scots Guards stemmed the tide. Shortly afterwards Lieutenant Colonel Viscount Gort DSO, MVO, MC (he would subsequently win the Victoria Cross and in the Second World War commanded the BEF in

Bourlon station as it looked in 1913. A. Boyer

1940 in France) commanding the 4th Grenadier Guards, came up to find Lieutenant Colonel Plunkett and to offer his assistance. He was asked to lead his Battalion to the sunken road running north from Anneux Chapel and to reinforce the flank if needed. In fact they were not required, but the column was heavily shelled by the observant Germans. The additional strength from the Guards gave Plunkett's command the reinforcements it needed; in the hours of daylight all enemy attacks were beaten off with heavy losses and these attacks gradually died down. In the village Lieutenant Colonel Warden's hold on the south corner was strong; all the approach streets to his redoubt were choked with dead Germans, though his building had been reduced to rubble. He moved his HQ to a dugout behind it. The village effectively belonged to the enemy except for the southern and western parts. He knew the Division's relief would be arriving later on the 25th and was prepared to stay and wait for it. There were still no tanks and, whilst enemy attacks went on all day, it was a comparatively quiet day - apart from the incessant chatter of machine guns and bursting shells. The British dead in the wood and village could not be buried and were simply pushed out of the way, whilst the evacuation of the hundreds of wounded was almost an impossibility if they could not walk.

On the left of the Bourlon front the 36th Division was also spending an inactive day, their relief was almost due. Beyond them the 56th Division, which had been ordered to recapture part of the Hindenburg Support System, had attacked at 1pm. Despite local success, it was repeatedly counter attacked; by night the front trench was held to a point on the Inchy road and they were still in contact north of Tadpole Copse.

Bourlon station as it looked in 1918. A. Boyer

In the meantime the Guards Division, in its 4,400 yard front from Cantaing to the eastern edge of Bourlon Wood, though constantly shelled, was not attacked and spent the day digging in on the eastern edge of the wood and immediately in front of Fontaine.

At 2.30pm Brigadier General Bradford VC, commanding 186 Brigade of the 62nd Division, arrived at Lieutenant Colonel Plunkett's battered 119 Brigade HQ in the red bricked chalet to discuss the relief by the battalions of the Duke of Wellington's Regiment. They began to arrive at 5.30pm and the weary men of 119 Brigade disentangled themselves from the undergrowth and shallow trenches they had dug. They were met by guides, as so difficult had their time been most of them had no idea which way was out. All evening the enemy remained active, the Dukes going into battle as soon as they arrived. Shelling was severe and casualties in the last few hours as men got out of their protective holes to walk away were numerous. The evacuation of the wounded was particularly dreadful, as many could not be moved. Before midnight the Scots Guards, 12th SWB, 19 RWF, 17th, 18th Welch, 14th Argylls, 11th Kings Own and 15th Hussars were heading south westerly out of the wood to Anneux. In front of Bourlon village Brigadier General R.O'B. Taylor's 187 Brigade arrived at the same time and those battalions of (or attached) to 121 Brigade started to come away, with the exception of the two Cavalry Dismounted Battalions, who would stay in support.

The Yorkshire men of the York and Lancs and the King's Own Light Infantry had no knowledge of the whereabouts of Lieutenant Colonel Warden's East Surreys, but at 2.40pm on the 26th a runner from 121 Brigade found him. His orders were to maintain his position in the south of the village until tanks would arrive to escort the H.L.I. and others trapped in the village to safety. He was given no idea when this event would take place – in any case he considered that it was unlikely to happen at all. In fact, by 8.30am on the 27th, there was no sign of them.

Another day had passed and Sir Douglas Haig's objectives were not achieved. He now put pressure on General Byng and issued a new instruction to him, signed by Lieutenant General L.E. Kiggell, his Chief of Staff. It began, 'In confirmation of verbal instructions already given', and then went on to tell him to secure without delay ground already won on the flanks and front of Bourlon Wood. Haig reckoned that there was sufficient artillery and he now had two fresh divisions, the 2nd and 47th, at his disposal as well as the Cavalry Corps. To General Sir William Robertson, the CIGS in London, he sent a telegram confirming his instructions, stressing again the importance of Bourlon Hill. The Hon. Sir Julian Byng could no longer be in any doubt that a lot was expected of him.

It is true that Lieutenant General Sir Charles Woollcombe's IV Corps report received by Byng at 6.45pm contained no definite information regarding the situation at Bourlon. But it was obvious another great effort had to be made if the Germans were to be driven clear of the wood, the village and the shoulder of the ridge.

At 11.35pm Byng despatched an order to Woollcombe,

> *To capture not later than Tuesday 27th of November the villages of Fontaine and Bourlon, the line defined as extending along the northern slope of the ridge beyond the two villages and Bourlon Wood.*

Sir Douglas Haig's order had certainly put the cat amongst the pigeons.

The casualties to the battalions of the 40th Division were horrific. Of the 12th SWB not many were left to walk out of the wood, ten officers and 123 other ranks were killed or missing, 12 officers and 243 other ranks were wounded. The 19th RWF, who had gone into the wood with them on the 23rd, had suffered almost as badly, with nine officers and 30 other ranks killed, nine officers and 237 other ranks wounded and 85 others missing. The Scots Guards, who had only entered the wood the previous day, had four officers killed and wounded and 91 other ranks. The 13th East Surreys, who would not leave Bourlon until midday on the 27th, had casualties of six officers and 233 other ranks. Major General Ponsonby's 40th Division left the battle scene (mostly on the night of the 25th and the early hours of the 26th) with total casualties of 172 officers and 3,191 other ranks killed, wounded and missing. The eighty decorations for valour give little indication of the tremendous heroism exhibited by the Division as a whole in the

hell of the fighting in the wood and village: positions which an equally brave enemy had no intention of conceding. In fact only one other Division in the whole of the Cambrai battle suffered more; the 29th Division in its battles at the St Quentin Canal had 184 officers and 4,234 casualties in total but these occurred over a fourteen day period. The fighting in Bourlon Wood became a symbol for the Division of its resolve and determination, and an acorn and oak leaf was incorporated into the Divisional sign.

26th November

It was another cold and windy morning but action within Bourlon Wood and the village was muted. Certainly there was rifle and machine gun fire but the Germans, fought almost to a standstill, needed rest. They made no infantry attack during the day, though their artillery continued at intervals to pound the wood and the approaches to it at Graincourt and Anneux.

The Royal Flying Corps bombed bridges over the Sensée River five miles to the north and at 10am the heavy artillery began a deliberate bombardment of Fontaine Notre Dame, Quarry Wood, Moeuvres, Inchy and Sains-lès-Marquion. The 36th Division on the left flank could only shelter from the horizontal blizzard of fire that swept the country. The bombardment, for some unknown reason, was totally inadequate at Fontaine; only twelve 6" howitzers fired on it, whilst Bourlon village was left untouched because of British troops thought to be in there. Lieutenant Colonel Warden's 13th East Surreys were in both part of the village and the northern part of the wood and would be until just before dawn the following day.

The most important event of the day was the high level conference in a hut at Havrincourt. Without doubt the Commander-in-Chief's actions of the previous day had stirred everyone who was present. It was attended by Lieutenant General Woollcombe, Major Generals Feilding of the Guards Division and Braithwaite of the 62nd. The conference began at 9.30am. At 11am Sir Julian Byng arrived, closely followed by the Commander-in-Chief. The subject was the following day, the 27th. The plan was that two divisions, the 62nd and the Guards, would attack eastwards, capturing Bourlon and Fontaine, and consolidate a line along the northern slopes of Bourlon Ridge. Byng went over his plan. There would be twelve tanks with the Guards in their attack on Fontaine and a further twenty with the 62nd at Bourlon. At the outset, before the arrival of Sir Julian Byng, General Fielding was already aware of what was proposed because of a visit to him by

Brigadier General H.D. de Pree from IV Corps staff. He had already written his objections to the plan. Fontaine was well defended, his Division would be advancing across open ground into a salient, open on three sides to artillery fire from high ground at Rumilly, south of Fontaine, and beyond the Bourlon Ridge and Cambrai. Its frontage was 4,000 yards which, if the attack succeeded, would be increased by a further 1,800 yards. It was essential that the village should be reduced to rubble. In addition, he only had six fresh battalions, and his Division had suffered 3,000 casualties only six weeks earlier at Ypres. Why should, he argued, the capture of Bourlon be easier now after the Germans had got organised? It would be better to withdraw entirely from the low ground and build a defence line on the Flesquières Ridge. His logic was sound and a few days later the British would do exactly that. Woollcombe had listened to Feilding without comment, except to say that it would have to be a matter for Byng. Feilding knew his case was hopeless when Byng outlined the plan once more. Sir Douglas Haig appeared to understand Fielding when he, Haig, said there would be no extension of the offensive operation but that the attack would probably enable the main objective to be captured, the best line for the winter. In any case there were no more reserves to do more than that. He then rode off to study the prospects from Flesquières Ridge. The meeting broke up; the attack the following day would take place. No one had voiced the obvious question, what was to be done with Bourlon and Fontaine if captured? Haig had said there were no reserves with which to hold them.

It certainly seemed to all that this was the end of the C-in-C's original hopes. His thoughts that morning, sitting on his horse in the blizzard, looking across the open land to the menacing bulk of Bourlon Hill, littered with broken equipment, tanks and thousands of men and animals moving about or encamped, must have been grim. He had failed.

The two divisional commanders went back to their Headquarters, for there was no time to waste. Zero hour would be at 6.20am, the formal operation order was issued at 5pm, and meanwhile the snow continued unabated. The prospects for the already cold and wet infantrymen were poor.

As for the enemy, by now they had seven divisions on a 10,000 yard arc from Inchy to Bourlon with more than 500 guns, 118 of them heavies. With the arrival of the Guards Division they knew a British attack was imminent. Lieutenant General von Moser had now positioned the 221st Division and the 119th in line at Fontaine, with the 49th on its way. The British two divisions would have more than 200 guns, of which 76 were heavies and mediums, but the bad weather and road conditions might yet reduce this total.

On his return to his HQ General Feilding held a meeting confirming with his brigadiers the plan to attack Fontaine which, perforce, could only be simple. Four battalions would take part from Brigadier General Sergison-Brooke's 2 Brigade, now in reserve at Ribècourt, on a 2,000 yard attack line. On the left would be the 2nd Irish Guards, immediately north of the Fontaine - Bourlon track on the eastern side of the wood, and some 500 yards into it. On their right would be the 1st Coldstream Guards, below the track and almost out of the trees; and on their right the 3rd Grenadiers, in the open and either side of the main road at the western entrance to Fontaine. The 1st Scots Guards would hold the right of the line. The attack would have twelve tanks. Thus far Fontaine had been hardly touched by shell fire. The first objective was a line running south to north through the village, past the church and across to the railway, west of the station, and which then bent back to the north of Bourlon Wood. The second objective was the railway station and the east part of Fontaine. When all this was achieved they were to throw an outpost line round the village.

General Braithwaite's Yorkshire men, already in Bourlon village and the wood, would have twenty tanks but no artillery bombardment because British troops were already there - but no one knew exactly where. Lieutenant Colonel Warden learnt that his men were on the line for a selective barrage and so pulled his East Surreys further back.

At dusk the thirty-two tanks set out from Ribécourt but this time the tank crews' enthusiasm was dimmed with their experience of too many attacks unsupported by infantry. The crews guessed it would be the same this time. The journey from Ribécourt to the battle line, in the dark and a blizzard, was enough to dampen anyone's spirit and further they were aware that the enemy was waiting for them.

On this day, whilst Sir Julian Byng was holding his conference, so was Crown Prince Rupprecht with General von der Marwitz at Le Cateau. They ware preparing for another one with Ludendorff on the morrow, to confirm their counter stroke, the first major offensive against the British since 1915.

Chapter Four

THE FINAL ATTEMPT TO CAPTURE BOURLON VILLAGE, BOURLON HILL AND FONTAINE NOTRE DAME

27th November, Tuesday

The snow had turned to icy rain. The attack would begin at 6.20am along the whole line, going from the 3rd Grenadier Guards (600 yards west of Fontaine Church and across the main road, just before the factory), through the 1st Coldstream north of them, with their left flank in the eastern edge of the wood. From there the line crossed the sunken road from Fontaine to Bourlon, with the 1st Irish Guards on the left, but further back into the trees. The whole Guards' attack aimed north-east towards the railway line skirting Fontaine's eastern edge. Immediately on the left of the Irish Guards began Major General Braithwaite's 62nd Division. Brigadier General Bradford's 186 Brigade of men from the Duke of Wellington's was on the right, next to the Irish Guards; its task was to clear the northern part of Bourlon Wood and the long narrow length of the eastern part of the village to the railway. Brigadier General R.O'B Taylor's 187 Brigade of York and Lancs and KOYLI would clear the main portion of the village. To both Brigades was attached a West Yorkshire Regiment Battalion, the 2/7th and 2/8th from Brigadier General Viscount Hampden's 185 Brigade. Both villages were strongly defended, particularly Bourlon, where the Germans had built strong barricades across the streets, with 77mm field guns hidden behind them, able to fire at close range at both tanks and infantry.

During the hours of darkness of the night of the 26th and 27th all the battalions struggled forward into their positions for Zero hour, in particular those Yorkshiremen and Irish Guards who had to get through the wood and deep mud which the ground had become. Keeping in touch was almost an impossibility and the difficulty of trying to dig in amongst the tree roots with only the lightweight entrenching tool forced many to simply lie down and use whatever depression was available. German shelling had not stopped, as they knew that something was afoot; whilst there were still many Germans holed up in the wood, amongst and behind the British infantry. As the Irish Guards reached the south edge of the wood they were caught by the

77

barrage and forty casualties resulted. Lieutenant Colonel the Hon. Harold Alexander, the Irish Guards commander, was already concerned as to whether his Battalion would arrive strong enough for the attack. He would survive to become a distinguished Field Marshal in the Second World War, better known as (Earl) Alexander of Tunis.

62nd (West Riding) Division's battle.

Each Brigade had a frontage of 1,000 yards. At 6.20 a special bombardment began, half shrapnel and high explosive, on the main portion of the village, 187 Brigade's battle arena, lifting 200 yards each ten minutes. The KOYLIs and York and Lancs started well behind the tanks, of which there were nineteen for both Brigades (the promised 20th had broken down). On the left, eleven of them led the 2/5th York and Lancs into the village from the south and four protected the Brigade's left flank by attacking machine gun posts in the Marquion Line. On reaching the village they ran into the German barricades, almost untouched by the barrage. The tanks suffered badly and ten

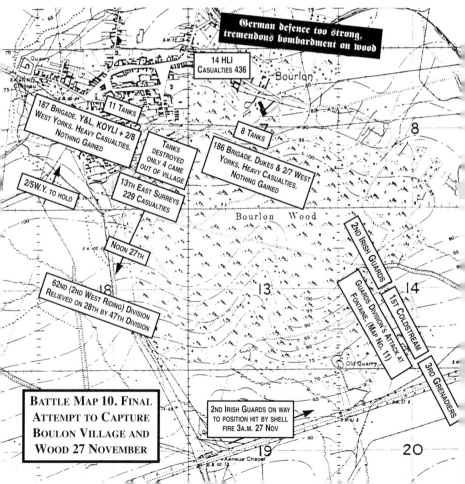

BATTLE MAP 10. FINAL ATTEMPT TO CAPTURE BOULON VILLAGE AND WOOD 27 NOVEMBER

were quickly disabled, in fact five out of nineteen were totally lost and never seen again. The 2/5th KOYLIs suffered badly from rifle and machine gun fire, coming into them in enfilade. In the hours before the Battalion was withdrawn it had taken more than 300 casualties. There was no sign of the HLI in the village, only their dead. In the meantime Lieutenant Colonel Warden's East Surreys, those last to leave of the 40th Division, assembled under cover near his obliterated red brick chalet HQ and, in small parties, each with an officer or NCO, came away from the hell they had endured, heading back to Graincourt.

On the right of the attack Brigadier General Bradford's 186 Brigade of Dukes was checked by a strong machine gun position and veered to the left, to the main part of the village, unable to get to the long eastern arm, its principal objective. The railway could not be reached despite the help of three tanks. During the morning two of the male tanks had expended 200 rounds of six-pounder ammunition. At 4.30pm the inevitable counter attack began and the 2/7th Dukes were withdrawn from the eastern end of the village to the high ground in the rear. At mid morning Brigadier General R.O'B Taylor decided any further assault on the village would serve no purpose and so withdrew his Brigade to the crest of the western side of the wood and village. He brought up the 2/5th West Yorks from 185 Brigade to ensure the position would be secure.

Brigadier General Bradford's 186 Brigade was also withdrawn up the slope on the village's southern edge. Once again General Braithwaite's Division had come to a halt and could do no more. General von Moser, in the course of the morning, feared that the British had broken through his 3rd Guards Division at Fontaine and sent up the 221st Division in support, meanwhile ringing Bourlon Wood with a tremendous bombardment. Major General Braithwaite was told that his Division must hang on until, on the 28th, Major General Sir G.F. Gorringe's 47th Division would relieve him. This relief was duly carried out amongst a bombardment of gas shells. The Yorkshire Division in its second short time at Bourlon had suffered greatly: 79 officers and 1,565 other ranks killed, wounded or missing. The wood and village, which had never truly belonged to the British, had claimed from Yorkshire 154 officers and 3,178 other ranks.

The Guards Division.

From the start it was under a serious disadvantage, as the British artillery was denied permission to shell Cambrai, whence the German artillery could safely shell Fontaine. At Zero hour, 6.20am, the twelve tanks promised had not arrived, it was raining and an intense enemy barrage had begun along with that of the British. The battle for Fontaine was of a street fighting rarely seen in the war, men killing each other in the broken houses, behind walls and the ruins around the church 200 yards above the main street. Whilst the battle was in progress a German officer of the II/46th Reserve Regiment reported:

> *Armoured vehicles have entered Fontaine, whilst they can conquer high ground they cannot hold it. In the narrow streets they have no field of fire and are hemmed in, hand grenades tied together and thrown beneath them blow off their tracks. Our men have no fear and hunt with enthusiasm.*

The 2nd Irish Guards on the left flank, adjacent and close to 2/5th Duke of Wellington's, began their attack from about 700 yards south-west of the north-east corner of the wood. After a long march from Flesquières via La Justice and Graincourt and through the enemy barrage, they arrived in position at 5am with No. 4 Company, Captain A.E.F. Self MC of 1st Coldstream on their right. In front of the 'Micks' were concealed machine guns, whilst the earth constantly erupted from shell fire. Precisely at 6.20am, in the dark, they went forward behind the British barrage in two waves. Almost immediately they ran into a line of German posts and found many of the occupants sheltering from the elements at the bottom of the trenches. Many were quickly killed by the bayonet and those lucky enough to be allowed to surrender were sent to the rear as prisoners. By the end of the fight they had captured some hundreds of Germans, but most escaped because there were not enough men to guard them. As the advance continued, almost blindly in the brush, machine guns were captured but more men were lost. It

Captured Germans.

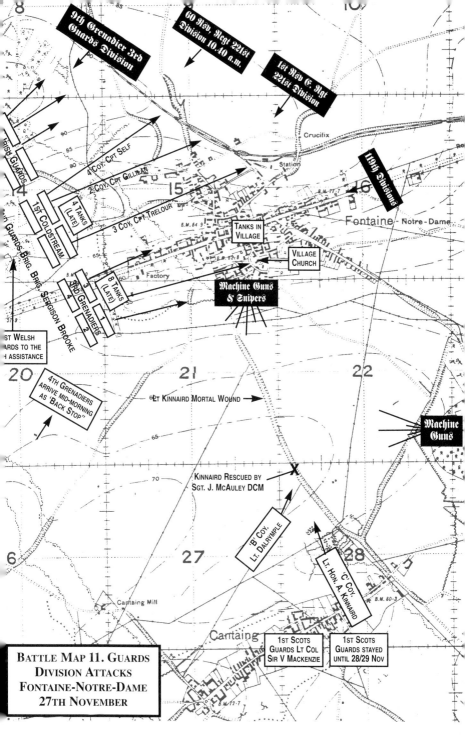

8

9th Grenadier 3rd Guards Division

60 Rsv. Regt 221st Division 10.40 a.m.

1st Rsv E. Rgt 221st Division

Crucifix

Station

19th Division

4 Coy. Cpt Self

2 Coy. Cpt Gillman

3 Coy. Cpt Trelour

Fontaine - Notre - Dame

Irish Guards

1st Coldstream

4 Tanks (Late)

Tanks in Village

B.M. 54 9

14

15

16

Village Church

Factory

3rd Grenadiers

8 Tanks (Late)

Machine Guns & Snipers

sh Guards-Brig. Brig. Sergison Brooke

1st Welsh Guards to the h assistance

20

4th Grenadiers arrive mid-morning as 'Back Stop"

21

6Lt Kinnaird Mortal Wound

22

Machine Guns

65

Kinnaird Rescued by Sgt. J. McAuley DCM

70

'B' Coy. Lt. Dalrymple

'C' Coy. Lt. Hon. A. Kinnaird

6

27

28

Cantaing Mill

B.M. 60 3

Cantaing

Battle Map 11. Guards Division Attacks Fontaine-Notre-Dame 27th November

1st Scots Guards Lt Col Sir V Mackenzie

1st Scots Guards stayed until 28/29 Nov

B.M. 12 7

was very difficult to maintain direction, the officers with compasses on the flanks having an impossible task. Within the first hour No. 2 Company had drifted to the left but the remainder maintained direction to the north-east corner of the wood, maintaining touch with the Coldstream. However by 9am, battered by shell fire and the tenacious enemy, they found the Battalion line had been penetrated in a number of places by the Germans and some had got behind them. Brigadier General Sergison Brooke learnt of this and ordered the 4th Grenadiers, in reserve, to send No. 2 Company (under Captain Britten) to the left flank. Whilst the Company was advancing Britten was wounded in the arm and Lieutenant H.W. Windeler was killed by a sniper. Second Lieutenant Oliver, commanding No. 3 Company, also going forward to plug holes in the Irish and Coldstream Line, was badly wounded in the chest whilst bringing in a wounded Irishman. The Battalion had now become split up into little fighting groups, the ferocious Irish Guards fighting for their lives. At midday Lieutenant Colonel Alexander had lost touch with his Battalion and the patrols he sent out could find no sign of them. Alexander feared it was going to be a total disaster. The Brigadier General also ordered the 1st Welsh Guards (Lieutenant Colonel Luxmoore Ball) to send two companies to their assistance. In fact, by no means were the Irish destroyed and they had somehow managed to maintain a Battalion front. They were very relieved when at dusk the Welshmen found them. The Irish guards came out of the Wood only 117 strong. Later, at the count in Ribécourt, they assessed the total casualties as 322, nine of them officers. Only Alexander, his second in command, Captain the Hon W.S. Alexander, his Adjutant, Captain Nugent, his assistant, Captain Sassoon and two others were unhurt.

1st Coldstream's front was only 250 yards but, at its final objective, 1,200 yards away, this fanned out to a 2,000 yard width. Captain Self's No. 4 Company was to seize the high ground north of Fontaine, Captain Treloar DSO (No. 3 Company) would press through the north part of the village and occupy the railway station, preserving contact with the 3rd Grenadiers on the right. Captain Gillilan's No. 2 Company would attack between them in the centre and No. 1 Company (Lieutenant Newland MC) split into four would mop up and support the flanks. They had got into position safely despite the foul weather. At 6.20am they started off without any tanks and quickly ran into difficulties with fire from the many Germans in well dug trenches and houses, in a sunken road facing them and in the many small sandpits that abounded on the north side of the village. No. 4 Company was pushed north by the heavy fire and became isolated from the rest. It pressed on to the first objective, about 300 yards west and north of the railway station. Although they captured fifty prisoners, they were themselves reduced to only forty all ranks. At this point the company was ordered to retire else it would have been wiped out. They abandoned the two 77mm field guns they had overrun but brought in their prisoners, some of whom were carrying the Coldstream's wounded. By 10am they were back at the start line. The other two companies, Captains Treloar's No. 3 and Gillilan's No. 2, pressed on into the village. No. 2 lost all its officers and sergeants except Gillilan, but arrived at the railway cutting with 200 hundred prisoners to its credit. Due to enfilading fire it could not get in touch with No. 4 - which in fact had withdrawn. Captain Treloar's men, after a severe struggle, drove the enemy out of a trench on the north-western front of Fontaine and then surged forward, bombing the cellars, but there were not enough of them to mop up properly. They forced their way to the railway, seizing the line and the station, capturing three more field guns, some machine guns and more prisoners and contact with the 3rd Grenadiers on the right was held. Because of the situation on the right, at 10.40am the Brigade commander ordered the Coldstream to fight their way back to the start line. Only 180 answered their names; amongst the dead was the 20 year old Second Lieutenant Charles Fletcher Hartley, who was born in the USA but had been educated at Harrow.

On the right of the attack, as the barrage began at 6.20am, the ground east of Fontaine was swept with machine gun fire to dampen the German barrage coming from La Folie Wood. The 3rd Grenadiers did not advance until 6.45am; once more the tanks were late, but they arrived soon afterwards. The two companies (1 and 2) advancing south of the main road were in trouble as soon as they set out, coming under heavy machine gun fire from La Folie Wood, only 1,000 yards south of the village. In the initial bombardment the wood had hardly been touched by the gunners. All the six officers, most of the NCOs and the majority of the men were struck down. One sergeant and six men found their way to the church 600 yards away. They were joined by others from Numbers 3 and 4 Companies; by 7.45 a.m. they were fighting with an overwhelming number of Germans, who poured out of the houses and cellars, whilst some used two derelict tanks as strong points. Of the eight tanks that had entered the village, three were lost. The enemy had attacked the tanks fearlessly, climbing on top of them, shooting into what holes they could find, being 'hosed' off by other tanks. At 7am, when things appeared to be going well for the 2nd Guards Brigade and the barrage had paused for thirty minutes, Lieutenant Colonel Sir V. Mackenzie decided it was time to send in 'C' Company of the 1st Scots Guards. They came out of the sunken road from Cantaing leading to the southern corner of Fontaine. The ground provided absolutely no cover except in the sunken road; but they could crawl and avoid the murderous fire from La Folie Wood. This they did successfully, but as they approached the southern side of Fontaine, where the houses remained full of Germans (the Grenadiers would never totally clear them), machine gun fire hit the Scots. Their casualties mounted very quickly so that they were stopped about 150 yards short of the village; and thereby could not assist the Grenadiers. Lieutenant the Hon. Arthur Kinnaird lead the Company, but was first hit in the leg and then, as he turned, hit again, in the back. The other two officers, Lieutenants A.M. Scott and Hon. J.A. Burn, were also wounded and put out of action. Sergeant John McAulay, DCM, seeing the seriously wounded Kinnaird, went to his side, bringing him back for 400 yards into the sunken road, and got him into a dugout. He was himself knocked down twice by shell fire and killed two Germans as he retired with the dying Kinnaird. John McAulay had been a miner then a Glasgow policeman and a heavyweight boxer of note before joining the army. Despite his tremendous efforts, he was still not

Bringing wounded up from a dugout on stretchers by winch, 1917.

finished. He took command of the Company and successfully repulsed an attack on the left; aided by two men with a machine gun he killed at least fifty of the enemy. He was awarded the Victoria Cross (Gazetted 11 January 1918) and survived the war, dying in Glasgow in 1956.

Reinforcements from B Company were sent up with Lieutenant Dalrymple to command both C and the survivors of B. Withdrawing deeper into the sunken road, the Scots Guards stayed there until told to retire during the night of the 28th/29th. The casualties in just these two Companies were four officers, three of them wounded, and seventy-three other ranks, 21 of those killed.

By 1pm the battle for Fontaine was over. The Guards were back where they had started. The 4th Grenadiers arrived at midmorning to stop any hope the Germans might have of advancing west of the village. The casualties were heavy: 2 Guards Brigade had suffered a total of 38 officers and 1,043 other ranks. Uniquely, the Guards Division had lost a battle.

In the afternoon General Byng, learning of the attack's failure, gave IV Corps orders to cease the offensive, 'The 3rd Army has no more resources at its disposal'. In the confirmation order of the same day he ordered the 62nd Division to be relieved by the 47th, Major General Gorringe, and the Guards by the 59th (2nd North Midland) Division, Major General C.F. Romer. All tanks would be withdrawn and were not to be used any further on IV Corps front. Field Marshal Sir Douglas Haig's campaign for Cambrai was over. No one could view it with satisfaction; the events of the past seven days had been of failed attacks, albeit filled with bravery and stubborn endeavour. Perhaps the enemy's strength had been consistently underestimated. The outcome was such that, although the highest part of the ridge and hill had been won, the enemy still looked down from the shoulders of the ridge upon the British positions on the Cantaing-Anneux-Graincourt plain.

What was not known by the British was that on this day at Le Cateau Prince Rupprecht and Ludendorff were confirming the plans for the great counter stroke to regain all the lost territory of the *Siegfried Stellung*. Not only that: they were also considering the possibility of trapping the bulk of the British forces before they could retire west of Havrincourt and Metz-en-Couture. The attack could not begin before the 30th, as Rupprecht's forces could not all be in place; but he thought himself fortunate that the British attacks were confined to the Bourlon front, and hoped that they might continue a little longer, further dissipating British strength and ammunition resources.

Chapter Five

THE CALM BEFORE THE STORM
28th - 29th November

The whole length of the salient into the German line achieved during the eight-day battle was nine miles long and four deep, from Bourlon Wood southwards to beyond Bantouzelle. Lieutenant General Sir W.P. Pulteney's III Corps held the southern sector from just south of Ribécourt and the Flesquières Ridge. Lieutenant General Sir C.L. Woollcombe's IV Corps was responsible from there to north of the main road, the Canal Du Nord at the broken main road bridge north west of Graincourt and up to Moeuvres, a total of some 5,000 yards. The depth of IV Corps' salient from the dry canal to Cantaing was about 8,000 yards. The deepest bulge to the north encompassed Bourlon Wood. The southern, III Corps' sector, is fully covered in *Cambrai: The Right Hook* in this series. Because the whole of Bourlon Ridge had not been won it lacked the security General Byng would have liked; but within hours he would have three fresh divisions in the line there, the 59th and the 47th, with the 2nd behind them at the Canal Du Nord. Further behind the 2nd Division, north of the main road facing Moeuvres, was the 56th Division and then Major General C.J. Deverell's 3rd Division (known as the Iron Division) to its left. This latter Division had so far taken no part in the battle for Bourlon Wood; but in the subsequent German attack it became involved on the extreme left, west of Tadpole Copse. Two miles south of the 59th, west of Noyelles, was the 6th Division of III Corps. Sir Julian Byng felt reasonably content about the strength of the position, and there was a good proportion of the Third Army's heavy artillery supporting them.

The weather on the 28th had become milder. A lot of information about German troop movement by road and rail was received: GHQ expected an attack on the Bourlon Front but had no doubt it would contain it; in any case it was thought the German losses in Flanders and here at Cambrai had exhausted them. How wrong could GHQ Intelligence have been? So confident were they that the 36th Division was sent west to the Drocourt-Quéant line, the *Wotan Stellung*, and V Corps (Lieutenant General Sir A.E. Fanshawe) was ordered to relieve IV Corps on the Bourlon Front at 3pm on the 30th. The Ninth Wing of the RFC departed to the north of the Third Army. Not all of the senior officers were so sanguine. Lieutenant General Sir Thomas D'O Snow, commanding VII Corps in the south, tried to arouse Army HQ at Albert to a sense of emergency; he warned his own divisions in the south of the 'Flanders Sanatorium' of possible enemy action.

Meanwhile, in the Bourlon Sector on the 28th, General von Moser's Arras Group began an intensive bombardment of Bourlon Wood, pouring 16,000 rounds of gas and high explosive into it. This was at a time when the 47th Division was taking over from the 62nd, so that casualties were high in both divisions. The more experienced soldiers wondered why the Germans had not used the deadly mustard gas. Some felt that it was because the Germans would be attacking here soon, as mustard gas was dangerous for days afterwards.

It was during this bombardment that the only Victoria Cross, was won in all the fighting at Bourlon. Private George William Clare was a stretcher bearer of the (dismounted) 5th (Royal Irish) Lancers, who were holding the line during the divisional take over. He fearlessly carried out his care for the wounded lying on the battlefield and dressed and conducted wounded over the open to the dressing station 500 yards away. At one point, when he saw that the garrison of a post in the open 150 yards ahead were all casualties, he crossed the machine gun and rifle fire swept open ground, dressed the wounded and then manned the post alone. He then carried a badly wounded man back to

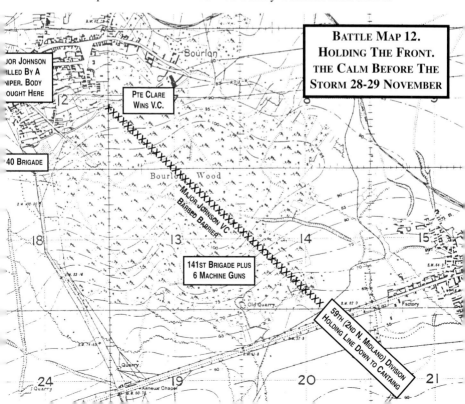

BATTLE MAP 12.
HOLDING THE FRONT.
THE CALM BEFORE THE
STORM 28-29 NOVEMBER

the dressing station. There he was told that gas shells were falling in profusion in the valley below; and the gas was being blown towards our line of trenches and occupied shell holes. He set out to warn the occupants, all the time under shell fire; eventually he was killed by one of the shells. His body was not recovered.

On the 28th, despite the bombardment, it was decided to strengthen the line at Bourlon Wood and the Royal Engineers were called upon to build a double apron barbed wire barricade. During the night the 229th and 231st Field Companies, assisted by the Sappers and Pioneers of the 40th Division and with the 12th Green Howards, the Pioneers from the 62nd Division, set to work. They were detailed to erect a 1,200 yards length, running diagonally across the wood down to the south east corner at the main road, in front of Fontaine. Much of the material was German from their dump at Anneux chapel, which had been intended for the strengthening of the *Siegfried Stellung*. The wire was carried up in 56lb rolls slung on a pole by two men, who were already tired out. The work took four and a half hours and many casualties were suffered in the operation. One of them was Major Frederick Henry Johnson VC, aged 27, who commanded the 229th Company. He had won his Victoria Cross as a Second Lieutenant in September 1915 in the attack on Hill 70 at Loos. He was shot in the neck by a sniper. His body was brought back to a house near to the ruined Chateau but lost during subsequent fighting. He is commemorated on the Memorial to the Missing at Louverval. His VC was purchased in 1983 by the former minister, Alan Clark, who wrote a book largely about Loos.

On the 29th, a quiet day everywhere, Lieutenant General Snow in the south warned his divisions to be on high alert, much movement having been seen of infantry, artillery and aircraft by RFC observers. His fears were communicated to Sir Julian Byng, but they did not unduly alarm him. In the afternoon of the 29th the three Tank Brigades lined up in Havrincourt Wood to be inspected by Brigadier General Elles. His force

had suffered grievously in the battle, 188 officers and 965 other ranks were killed wounded and missing, with more than 350 of the original tank force put out of action, destroyed, disabled or broken down. Thanking them for their heroic effort, he left for his Headquarters; the tanks went as well, going back into the Somme at Bray and Méaulte, near Albert, Third Army's HQ.

Frederick Henry Johnson.

The night passed peacefully and the great downpouring of poison gas drifted away in the wind. Despite the heavy bombardment, a sense of relaxation

Outpost man. Note the periscope. The fixed bayonet denotes that he is in a forward postion.

prevailed. Sir Julian Byng's rank of General had been confirmed and he was dining in some splendour in Albert. However his men were not, regimental officers were struggling to get some sort of hot meal to them in the battered, cold and wet trenches of the front line at Bourlon and Fontaine. A major concern for them was the shortage of men. At the outset a battalion could perhaps have 600 bayonets available but now they were lucky if they could muster 200 fighting men.

The battle arena of IV Corps at Bourlon was only about four square miles and many men and animals were crammed into this small space. It was all, however, strangely quiet. No one understood it after the previous hectic week, but they settled down to improve their trenches, dug outs, wiring and weapons, all thinking, hopefully, that the Germans had suffered enough. In various places wounded were recovered, some of whom had been lying out for days and would die because of this. The many dead were left to melt away in the undergrowth.

No one misread the quietness. All were well aware of enemy movements in and about Cambrai. Of all of the officers, the two dozen battalion commanders had the most to do, anticipating and preparing for the enemy and inspiring their men to alertness.

Chapter Six

THE GERMAN COUNTER STROKE AND THE END OF THE BATTLE OF CAMBRAI

30th November to 7th December

The German plan for the attack, to start on Friday, 30 November, the details of which were thrashed out at the conference at Le Cateau (Headquarters of Second Army), was breathtaking in its concept. General von Kathen's Busigny Group (which consisted of thirteen divisions) would attack in the south with General von Watter's Caudry Group of five divisions and would move westwards. Two divisions of Kathen's Group would make the initial attack, the 208th and the 183rd, followed by the 34th, 28th, 220th, 30th and the 9th Reserve from Watter's Group. They were all fresh and could count on massive support. Crown Prince Rupprecht's first blow would come up from the south east and would strike against VII Corps, towards Epèhy, six miles below the Gouzeaucourt - Bonavis Road, rolling up the British to Metz-en-Couture and Havrincourt. Assuming that went well, Lieutenant General von Moser's Arras Group (214th, 221st, 49th and 21st Reserve Divisions, plus the 3rd Guards) would, on the same day, strike a hammer blow in the north between Moeuvres and Bourlon, against IV Corps. The 119th Division would attack westwards, south of Fontaine, driving IV Corps down across the Graincourt-Cantaing plain. Rupprecht regarded the recapture of the *Siegfried Stellung* frontal system as a minimum objective; his grander hopes were to smash Byng's Third Army. The attack in the northern sector was considered to be the main strike. Knowing the British were tired and that the Germans would have an overwhelming force, Rupprecht was confident of success. There were only three British divisions principally involved against it, all tired and depleted, but they would display the courage and bloody minded determination as characteristic of the British infantry as the German. The 'Uppercut', the attack in the south, is covered in *Cambrai: The Right Hook* in the same series.

The 'Hammer Blow' on the 30th November.

It was a fairly quiet day in the north, especially in Havrincourt Wood, in the early morning of that Friday. Almost all the tanks and men had left, there were only a few Tank Brigade staff left and at 9.30am the camp was empty. Colonel Arthur Courage, later Brigadier General, who had been badly wounded in the face at Ypres, was about to leave in his car when he heard sounds of machine gun fire and could see shells bursting uncomfortably close. He had thought the nearest enemy was six miles away. Then wounded men came straggling towards him who said the Germans had broken through at Gouzeaucourt. Brigadier General Hugh Elles received the news at 10am in his office at Albert. The half expected counter attack seemed to have started.

The Germans had also been firing steadily since dawn on the British batteries south of Graincourt and into Bourlon Wood with a usual mixture of phosgene gas and high explosives. A counter bombardment began but at 8.50am the Germans began a ferocious shelling of all the British front line from Moeuvres to Bourlon, in particular on the main Bapaume to Cambrai road, hitting the Sugar Factory and destroying some guns of the 255th Machine Gun Company of the 47th Division. The British had good observation north over the rolling, almost treeless land, west of Bourlon and the enemy

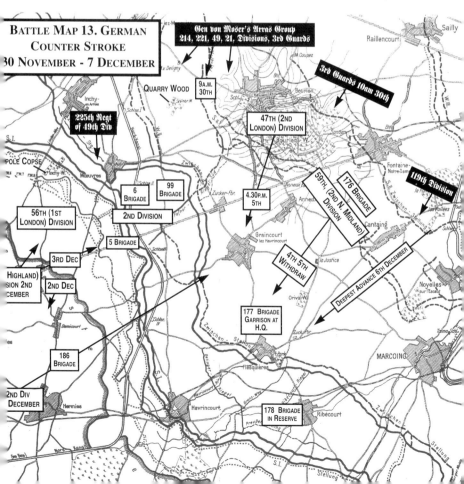

BATTLE MAP 13. GERMAN COUNTER STROKE 30 NOVEMBER - 7 DECEMBER

Gen von Moser's Arras Group 214, 221, 49, 21, Divisions, 3rd Guards

3rd Guards 10am 30th

QUARRY WOOD

9 A.M. 30TH

225th Regt of 49th Div

47TH (2ND LONDON) DIVISION

119th Division

6 BRIGADE

99 BRIGADE

176 BRIGADE

59TH, (2ND N. MIDLAND) DIVISION

2ND DIVISION

4.30 P.M. 5TH

56TH (1ST LONDON) DIVISION

5 BRIGADE

4TH 5TH WITHDRAW

3RD DEC

HIGHLAND) SION 2ND CEMBER

2ND DEC

DEEPEST ADVANCE 6TH DECEMBER

177 BRIGADE GARRISON AT H.Q.

MARCOING

186 BRIGADE

2ND DIV DECEMBER

178 BRIGADE IN RESERVE

could be seen concentrating a mile north west of Bourlon at Deligny Mill. The bombardment had set Cantaing ablaze and the Staffordshire battalions in the wood were badly hit by the gas.

The 59th (2nd North Midland) Division's story.

Not in the path of the German main attack, this Division was holding the right, the north-east, part of the British line from a point in Bourlon Wood on the track from Fontaine to Bourlon, then south to Cantaing, a 3,000 yard front. Brigadier General T.G. Copes's 176 Brigade, with the 2/5th North Staffords, was in the centre, about 1,500 yards south-west of Fontaine. Brigadier General T.W. Stansfield's 178 Brigade, the Sherwood Foresters, was in reserve at Ribécourt. When he learnt of the German 119th Division's attack at midday towards Marcoing, he sent two battalions and eight machine guns to Highland Ridge, which ran north-easterly from Flesquières, to help the 6th Division of III Corps to block any movement towards Graincourt. The other Brigade, 177 (Brigadier General C.H.L. James), was providing the garrison at Flesquières and with the 469th Field Company RE were already working on its defences; they would be the central point of the British 'fall back' line for the winter. The Germans' 46th and 58th Regiments [a German Regiment was the equivalent of a British brigade] of the 119th Division made two assaults out of Fontaine

towards Cantaing, one at 9am and the second at 11am. British artillery fire and the men of the 2/5th North Staffs broke up both these assaults. Before the first attack Lance Corporal J. Thomas of the centre battalion had gone forward to the edge of Fontaine to see what was happening, remaining out for three hours despite the German attack, killing several snipers and bringing back much information. He was awarded the Victoria Cross, survived the war and died in 1954.

**Lance Corporal
J. Thomas**

However the main thrust of the German attack of the day was to the Division's left. At 10.30am, as a precautionary measure, the artillery in the Graincourt valley was moved back and at 11.45am on 1 December the Division was ordered to garrison from the Hindenburg Support System to Flesquières. The night of the 30th/1st was quiet as far as infantry attacks were concerned as General Moser was too occupied with reorganising his troops for the attack in the morning; but his artillery continued to pound the wood whilst his infantry tried to infiltrate forward. The two battalions of Staffordshires, the 2/6th North Staffs and the 2/6th South

2/Lt F. G. Eckley's 'Fearnought'. He was killed in action on 27 November.

Staffs had suffered 688 casualties between them, necessitating their immediate relicf. The Division's work on that first day had been so successful that the 119th Division orders to secure Cantaing and the cross roads at La Justice, 2,000 yards to the west, had been foiled and it was too exhausted to continue. On 2 December Sir Douglas Haig, taking the longer view that the Germans would launch a large scale effort in the Spring, made the decision to pull back to his good winter line. Here, in the north, in the old IV Corps sector, that had now become V Corps, the line would pivot about Flesquières, coming up 1,000 yards from Ribécourt then, keeping to the high ground, after 'ringing' Flesquières, turn almost due west to the village of Boursies on the main road. On the 4th, the 59th Division withdrew its artillery behind the Flesquières Ridge. The 2/7th Sherwood Foresters of 178 Brigade and the 2/4th Lincolns of 177 provided the infantry holding the covering position at Cantaing, whilst the main bulk of the Division withdrew to man the Flesquières defences, securing its flank with trenches in Orival Wood. The withdrawal from Bourlon Wood was without incident. On the 6th, from daybreak, the enemy was very active, attacking Anneux towards Graincourt. They put a heavy barrage onto the Division. In the gloom of the winter afternoon, in the old 1914 style, some hundreds of closely packed infantry advanced on Orival Wood and Flesquières. At the cross roads north-east of the village some of the 104th and 107th Reserve Regiments, recently arrived from Russia, got into the Beet Factory, but were driven off by the 2/4th Lincolns and the 2/5th Leicesters, and some prisoners were taken. The British artillery now switched to this part of the winter line, practically destroying the German assault at Orival Wood. By the morning of the 7th the Division was firmly ensconced in its winter position at Flesquières. In the battle from 20 November to 7 December, the 59th Division had suffered 77 officer and 1,364 other rank casualties.

93

The 47th (2nd London) Division's story.

Two brigades were in Bourlon Wood and suffered greatly from the persistent gas and high explosive attack. On the right, in touch with the Staffordshire Brigade, was Brigadier General J.F. Erskine's 141st Brigade consisting of four battalions of the London Regiment. On the left were the 1/17th (Poplar and Stepney), with six guns of the 255th Machine Gun Company of 142nd Brigade; they would lose three of those guns to artillery fire later in the day. 140 Brigade (Brigadier General H.B.P.L. Kennedy) was almost out of the wood, lying mainly on the ridge at the west end, just below the village. 142 Brigade (Brigadier General V.T. Bailey) with the 1/22nd London (Queen's) were in reserve west of Flesquières, in the old Hindenburg trenches. The assault of General Moser's 3rd Guards Division (General von Lindquists) into the wood began at midmorning behind a phosgene gas attack. Even though the 1/19th (St Pancras) Battalion and the 1/6th and 1/15th

Brigadier General H.B.P.L. Kennedy.

Bourlon wood and village once more in German hands. The destroyed tanks in the foreground are probably from I Battalion.

London (Civil Service Rifles) who had been hurried forward, were forced backwards almost to the south-western edge, the strongly wired barrier built on the 28th helped greatly. The Germans could not take the wood just as the British had never taken the village. At nightfall they gave up. The London battalions were in a bad state but were still there; the 1/6th and 1/15th lost 300 men between them and the 1/19th was reduced to 9 officers and 61 other ranks. At 9am large bodies of troops were seen gathering in the open 1,000 yards north west in the area of Deligny Mill. General von Moser's force consisting of the 221st, the 241st and the 21st Divisions drive south, the 'Hammer Blow', was about to begin. Facing them was the 47th Division, already involved on the edge of Bourlon Wood and Major General C.E. Pereira's 2nd Division at the Cambrai - Bapaume main road above Graincourt. The 2nd Division's HQ was at Ytres, five miles south-west of Havrincourt Wood. In the morning three enemy observation balloons were flown from behind Bourlon village, the enemy bombardment intensified and the left of the attack, the 221st Division, whose target was Anneux and Graincourt, bore down on the 47th Division, aided by close support from aircraft. As would be seen later by the 59th Division, the old soldiers of the 47th Division saw massive blocks of infantry coming forward in waves. The British artillery of the 40th and 62nd Divisions, covering the front of the 47th Division, slew them in great swathes, but still they came on; rifles, Lewis guns

and Vickers machine guns took a great toll in the open, treeless ground. On the left of the Germans' attack 140 Brigade had the 1/6th London Rifles; on its left flank were the 1st Royal Berks (99 Brigade, 2nd Division), but they were not in close contact, so that the Germans were able to work round that flank. At 2pm their desperate, almost suicidal, assault overwhelmed four outposts of the 1/6th, driving two and a half companies off the ridge. This assault carried the Germans over the left rear of the 1/15th London (Civil Service Rifles), who were on the right, forcing them into a defensive position facing west along the edge of the wood. Counter attacked by the HQ Company of the 1/6th and the 1/8th (Post Office Rifles) the British regained some ground but not the ridge. By means of a further counter attack with the 1/15th they now succeeded in swinging forward to the left. Again the casualties had been high, the 1/6th losing 13 officers and 369 other ranks and the 1/15th 11 and 288. However, the 221st Division had been seriously hurt and its timetable for Anneux and Graincourt irretrievably disrupted. On 1 December, at 6pm, Lieutenant General Sir Edward Fanshawe's V Corps took over IV Corps sector, but for the moment this had no effect on the 47th Division. In fact after their setback on the 30th the Germans allowed the 47th Division a quiet day. Crown Prince Rupprecht received no news of his lack of success at Bourlon until 8pm; then he learned of the 214th and the Guards Divisions' exhaustion and so he ordered a halt for the 2nd to allow consolidation. Though there was some fighting in the southern sector, here at Bourlon both armies were using the cold winter day to recover; whilst the British readjusted to the new Corps requirements.

At 10am on the 2nd, V Corps artillery opened up on the enemy concentrations again, targeting the area north of Quarry Wood, between Bourlon and Moeuvres. The Germans replied with yet another bombardment on Bourlon Wood. At 8.10pm 140 Brigade, using 1/7th and 1/8th London Regiment, recovered its lost position on the ridge west of Bourlon. The night assault was by no means easy and the 1/7th lost heavily, some hundred casualties were caused by machine gun fire; but they did capture 50 prisoners and 16 machine guns.

On the 4th, in line with the 59th, the 47th Division received orders to fall back to the winter line. The last three battalions withdrew at 4.30am, whilst the 19 guns they had captured were destroyed. So skilfully was the withdrawal organised that the Germans did not immediately know they had gone. At last Bourlon Wood was empty of British troops. As the Division withdrew to Graincourt, the Engineers seriously damaged the catacombs under the church to make them useless to the Germans who would be allowed the village in the withdrawal plan. In fact the village would be commanded by the Division's machine guns from the high ground to the west of it. The only difficulty with the withdrawal came when the enemy finally realised that they were withdrawing. Marauding Germans, now advancing south of the main road, threatened to envelop the 47th's right flank. Once again the 1/15th Londons were in the thick of it; they lost 6 officers and about 100 other ranks, whilst the Brigade Machine Gun Company had to abandon six guns. By the morning of the 7th the Division was in position behind Hughes Trench and the Canal Du Nord, 2,000 yards west of Graincourt, their line for the winter. General von Moser could at last claim that terrible wood as his

Major General Gorringe's 47th Division had suffered 145 officers and 3,357 other rank casualties, just about the same as the 40th. The fighting at Bourlon Wood caused approximately 25% of the total British casualties at Cambrai; and about the same percentage to the valiant Germans.

Major General Gorringe.

The 2nd Division.

During the night of 26/27 November the 2nd Division, which had arrived by train from Flanders, marched east and relieved the 36th (Ulster) Division. Their position was astride the Canal du Nord, north-west of Graincourt and north of the main road near Lock No. 5, looking north to Moeuvres and the strong heavily wired *Siegfried Stellung*, the Hindenburg Line. To its right flank was the open, rising and almost treeless land, with the German held Quarry Wood 3,000 yards north and Bourlon Wood and the 47th Division a similar distance north-east. On the Division's left flank was the 56th (1st London) Division, with its three brigades, 167,168 and 169.

Just as did the men of the 47th Division, at about 9am on the 30th Pereira's men could see the Germans assembling for an attack in the area of Quarry Wood. These troops were the 358rd, 363rd and the 50th Infantry Regiments of General Brauchitz's 214th Division. Also present was the 21st Reserve Division (80th, 87th and 88th Regiments), part of the tremendous force which Rupprecht was sure would drive the British south to the Flesquières Ridge to be crushed by

97

the advance of his left attack, his 'uppercut'. In addition to the Divisional artillery was that of the 36th Division, which as normal in these battle circumstances, stayed behind when the rest of the Division was relieved; and the 93rd Army Field Brigade. Whatever mistakes of under estimation about the enemy that Sir Julian Byng might have made, it was not so here. The enemy would get a great shock this morning. Rarely had 9.2" Batteries had the satisfaction of firing on infantry and field guns in the open. A Battery of eight medium machine guns ranged on the attacking force poured 70,000 rounds into the massed ranks. Nevertheless the Germans were not stopped on the Division's right flank. 99 Brigade (Brigadier General R.O. Kellet) had the 1st Berks on its right, assisted by three Vickers guns of the 47th Division firing in enfilade. The Germans made some advances, posts were overrun in the old Hindenburg Line trenches, east of Lock No. 5, and two companies of the 23rd Royal Fusiliers were sent forward to help the Berkshires. At 12.30pm Brigadier General Kellett received a

Lock 5. South East of Moeuvres, 30th of November 1917. Looking towards Bourlon Wood. 17th Middlesex and 1st Kings Liverpools facing attacking Germans who were part of the 'Hammer Blow'.

report that the Germans had burst through as far as the Sugar Factory on the main road. In fact the news was false but Brigadier General W. Bulley-Smith sent the 2nd Ox and Bucks and the 24th Royal Fusiliers from his 5 Brigade up to counter attack if need be. On the left of the Berks, the 17th Royal Fusiliers (attached to 99 Brigade from 5 Brigade) were in a critical situation, under strong attack in the Hindenburg Support Line.

Captain Walter Napleton Stone, who commanded a company of the 17th Royal Fusiliers, isolated a 1000 yards in front of his Battalion, sent back valuable information as to the volume of the enemy in front of him. He was ordered to withdraw, leaving a rearguard to cover it. The attack developed with unexpected speed. Sending three platoons back, he stayed with the covering party. He was seen standing on the parapet of the trench, telephone in hand; when surrounded he cut the wire and with his men fought to the last until he was shot through the head and killed. He was awarded a posthumous Victoria Cross, but his body was not recovered.

Eventually a counter attack stopped the advance at the Hindenburg Support Line, barely a 1000 yards from the main road. To the left of

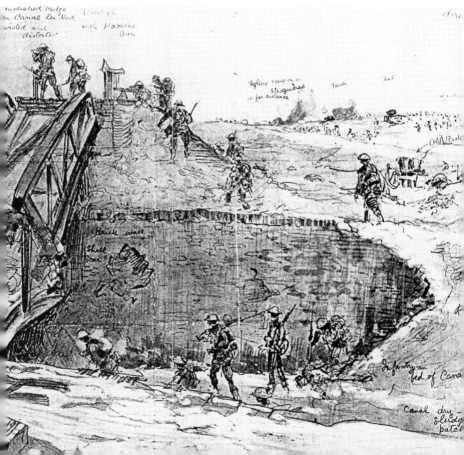

the 17th Royal Fusiliers were the 1st KRRC of 99 Brigade; with the assistance of eight machine guns, they devastated the German attack further, helped by the 6th and 242nd Machine Gun Companies who were, in fact west of the Canal du Nord near Lock No. 5. Further developments emphasise the huge volume of enemy infantry being deployed. At 11.45am 99 Brigade faced another mass assault. It was stopped by the Berkshires and Royal Fusiliers; but at 12.10am the British artillery was directed onto the Germans, smashing a second attack. Persistence eventually succeeded and at 2.30pm the Germans had driven in the left flank of the 47th Division. (The battleground was recaptured two days later and it was noted that 'the German dead lay so thick on the ground the British dead could not be seen'.) Finally on

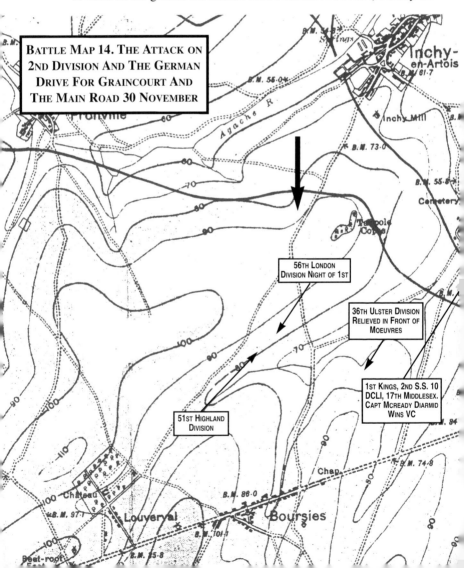

BATTLE MAP 14. THE ATTACK ON 2ND DIVISION AND THE GERMAN DRIVE FOR GRAINCOURT AND THE MAIN ROAD 30 NOVEMBER

56TH LONDON DIVISION NIGHT OF 1ST

36TH ULSTER DIVISION RELIEVED IN FRONT OF MOEUVRES

1ST KINGS, 2ND S.S. 10 DCLI, 17TH MIDDLESEX. CAPT MCREADY DIARMID WINS VC

51ST HIGHLAND DIVISION

the 30th at 4pm another strong attack was made on the 17th Royal
Fusiliers, but it was broken up by artillery fire; a trench in the
Hindenburg Line packed with Germans was utterly destroyed. The
Germans had done enough against 99 Brigade and stopped for the day.

Astride the Canal du Nord, 6 Brigade (Brigadier General R.K.
Walsh), holding the 2nd Division's left flank, had an equally hard day.
The 13th Essex occupied Canal Trench at Lock No. 5, on the eastern
side of the 'Ditch'. At 9.30am it was attacked but they managed to
drive the enemy off. At 10.30am the Germans put a box barrage around
the Lock and renewed their attack on Canal Trench, this time forcing
the 13th Essex out and capturing two Vickers guns in the process. The
men from Essex defended the trench until all their bombs and

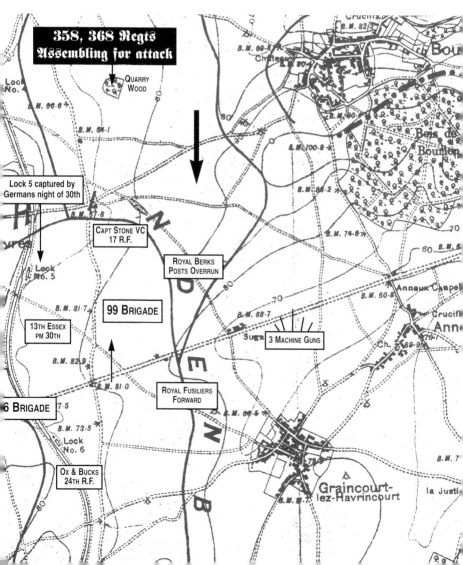

ammunition were expended. The 2nd South Staffs came up, but the Germans held onto Lock No. 5.

That same morning the 1st King's Liverpools held 6 Brigade's left flank in front of Moeuvres, in the Hindenburg Line trench, 1000 yards south of the village. The German attack developed from the shattered houses of the village and overwhelmed the right flanking company of the Battalion. Disregarding their heavy losses, the Germans kept coming until at 11am they were close to the Battalion HQ. The battle to stop them continued all day. The 17th Middlesex, part of the 2nd South Staffs and a company of the Division's Pioneers, the 10th DCLI, reinforced the Kingsmen. Captain Allastair McReady Diarmid, aged 29, of the Middlesex distinguished himself in the counter attacks. He was a bomber of great prowess, killing scores of the enemy, and enabling the defenders by the end of the day to secure the Brigade's old front line. On the following day during the resumed German attack he led his company forward through a heavy barrage, driving them back for 300 yards, and captured 27 prisoners.

Captain Allastair McReady Diarmid.

His absolute disregard for danger inspired his men; but he was eventually killed by a bomb. He was awarded a posthumous Victoria Cross. His body was never recovered. The German's advance on the 30th, which captured Lock No. 5, had also isolated a company of the 13th Essex, which had not been able to withdraw with the rest. All attempts to rescue them failed. After dark two runners made their way back to the Battalion to report that the two surviving officers, the CSM and platoon sergeants had agreed to fight to the death. The casualties to the Battalion in its battle at the Canal Du Nord amounted to 10 officers and 372 other ranks. In the morning the replacement of IV Corps by V Corps was postponed for twenty-four hours and at 11.45 am the 2nd Division was told to continue holding the line west of the dry canal. The 62nd Division, whose departure into rest had been cancelled, and two of its brigades were moved back towards the battle area, 185 Brigade from Beaumetz to two miles to the east at Hermies, attached to the 47th Division; and 186 Brigade, under Brigadier General R.B. Bradford, into the Hindenburg Support System southwest of Graincourt. He put his HQ in the dug (but dry) basin of Lock No 7, a mile south-west of the village. He was killed by a shell shortly after arriving. The highly respected and very young general was taken across the dry canal and buried in Hermies.

The German hopes of sweeping across the main road, on either side of the destroyed bridge, had thus far been frustrated. Nevertheless they did not cease in their attempt, and fighting continued on both sides of the canal during the night and would do so all day, on the 1st. At 11am the 1st King's Liverpools came under attack, but the Germans were driven off by Lewis gun and mortar fire. Two companies of the 2nd HLI, from 5 Brigade in reserve, helped to repulse an attack at mid afternoon on the western side; whilst on the eastern bank the Germans strove to break 6 Brigade's hold on Canal Trench. At 5pm the Brigade's front remained intact and prisoners were taken from the 225th Regiment of the 49th Reserve Division, which had now come down from north of Moeuvres. The pressure was certainly intense on the British left flank. Left of the 2nd Division was the 56th Division of VI Corps. During the night of the 1st, its exhausted battalions were relieved by the 51st (Highland) Division, brought back from Bapaume. The London Division's casualty count was much less than any other at the Bourlon front (45 officers and 694 other ranks). It had been in front of Inchy for six days, harassed by continual shell fire and the right wing of the German 49th Reserve Division.

On 2 December, at 10am, V Corps' heavy artillery opened up on the enemy concentrating north of Moeuvres and Quarry Wood. General von Moser had told Rupprecht that his divisions were too tired to make any large scale assaults; but his guns replied to the British for the whole of the afternoon. At 5pm 2nd HLI (5 Brigade), west of the Canal du Nord, was heavily attacked, but the assault came to nothing. The Highlanders and the artillery were able to drive them off; at one point, near the canal, the Germans had got into the HLIs position, but they were ejected with the bayonet. Similarly 99 Brigade, on the eastern bank, repulsed a German bombimg attack at Canal Trench.

On the night of the 3rd, the 51st Division relieved the left sector of 5 Brigade. On that morning Sir Douglas Haig had visited Sir Julian Byng at Albert and it was decided the withdrawal to the winter line would happen as quickly as possible. At 11pm on the 4th, 99 Brigade held the 2nd Division's front astride the Canal; but at daybreak on the 5th the Division was still under attack along both sides of the Canal. By the morning of the 7th it was clear of the main road and into the winter line, 2,000 yards south of the road, looking north. It had been in the front line of the left flank, in front of Moser's main thrust, and had suffered 85 officer and 2,156 other rank casualties.

All of Sir Douglas Haig's men were now settled into the winter line after a hard fought week of constant attack. Rupprecht's 'Hammer Blow' had failed.

The results of the battle measured in terms of ground gained or lost

A German gun pit captured by the tank in the background.

showed little profit. That part of the front due south of Marcoing to Demicourt represented an advance north-eastwards on a five mile front of two miles only. The Germans had made a similar inroad in the south about Gouzeaucourt. The wastage and strain to the Third Army must be taken into account. In total the British had employed fifteen infantry divisions and four of cavalry, more than a quarter of its total strength on the Western Front; and as many tanks, three Brigades, as could be assembled. The losses of all arms including the RFC, were more than 47,000. On the first day of the German Counter Stroke the British lost 6,000 prisoners and 168 pieces of artillery. The Germans used twenty Divisions, lost 11,000 prisoners, 140 artillery pieces and about 500 machine guns. Their casualties were about 53,000. The German morale was somewhat restored after the 'shock' of the first day and even the costly failure at Bourlon was seen as justified when the British retired to Flesquières and the 'Winter Line'. Nevertheless the Commander-in-Chief was perfectly right in principal; German divisions intended for Italy from the Russian Front had to be diverted to the Western Front. Also it is known that the number of German divisions on the Western Front increased in November by thirteen, due to arrivals from Russia. Long after the event Ludendorff asked what would have been the judgement on his Italian campaign if the British had exploited to the full their great initial success at Cambrai. The British held inquests as to whose fault it was that the attack at Cambrai had failed; officers were exonerated and blame was placed on a lack of training and perseverance. Haig shouldered most of the responsibility, but his final decision to withdraw to the strong line for the winter was sound, and its location was good; whilst his original reasons for embarking on the enterprise at all were fundamentally sound. Many lessons were learned, amongst them the value of unregistered shooting, the need for closer

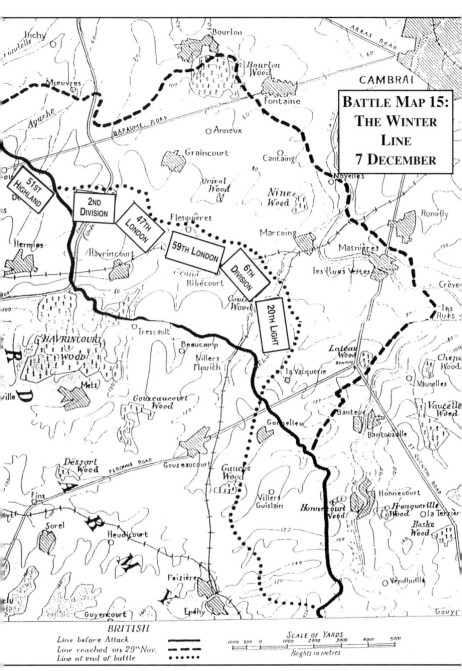

**BATTLE MAP 15:
THE WINTER
LINE
7 DECEMBER**

BRITISH
Line before Attack
Line reached on 29ᵗʰ Nov.
Line at end of battle

SCALE OF YARDS
1000 500 0 1000 2000 3000 4000 5000
Heights in metres

control by headquarters at all levels, and the essential need for the rapid
forward movement of troops in long ranging attacks. The new arm the
tank, despite its primitive nature, had done much to prove itself.

The shattered remains of two knocked-out tanks in Bourlon Wood.

51st (Highland) Division
Major General G.M. Harper

152 Brigade	**153 Brigade**	**154 Brigade**
(Brig.Gen. H.P. Burn)	*(Brig.Gen. A.T. Beckwith)*	*(Brig.Gen. K.G. Buchanan)*
1/6 Gordons	1/7 Black Watch	1/4 Gordons
1/6 Seaforths	1/5 Gordons	1/7 Argylls
1/8 Argylls	1/6 Black Watch	1/4 Seaforths
1/5 Seaforths	1/7 Gordons	1/9 Royal Scots
	1/8 Royal Scots (Pioneers)	

62nd(West Riding) Division
Major General W.P. Braithwaite

185 Brigade	**186 Brigade**	**187 Brigade**
(Brig.Gen. The Viscount Hampden)	*(Brig.Gen R.B. Bradford, VC)*	*(Brig.Gen. R.O'B Taylor)*
2/7 West Yorks	2/6 Duke of Wellington	2/4 K.O.Y.L.I
2/8 West Yorks	2/5 Duke of Wellington	2/5 York & Lancs
2/6 West Yorks	2/4 Duke of Wellington	2/4 York & Lancs
2/5 West Yorks	2/7 Duke of Wellington	2/5 K.O.Y.L.I.
	No Pioneers	

The 40th Division
Major General J. Ponsonby

119 Brigade	**120 Brigade**	**121 Brigade**
(Brig.Gen. F.P. Crozier)	*(Brig.Gen. The Hon C.S.H.D. Willoughby)*	*(Brig.Gen. J. Campbell)*
19 R.W. Fusiliers	14 Argylls	20 Middlesex
12 S.W. Borderers	14 H.L.Infantry	13 Green Howards
17 Welch Regt	11 King's Own	21 Middlesex
18 Welch Regt	13 East Surrey	12 Suffolk
	12 Green Howards (Pioneers)	

36th (Ulster) Division
Major General O.S.W. Nugent

107 Brigade
(Brig.Gen W.M. Withycombe)

108 Brigade
(Brig.Gen. C.R.J Griffith)

109 Brigade
(Brig.Gen. A.St Q. Ricardo)

107 Brigade	108 Brigade	109 Brigade
15 R.I. Rifles	9 R.I Fusiliers	10 R. Inniskilling Fusiliers
8 R.I. Rifles	13 R.I. Rifles	9 R. Inniskilling Fusiliers
10 R.I. Rifles	12 R.I. Rifles	14 R.I. Rifles
9 R.I. Rifles	11. R.I. Rifles	11 R. Inniskilling Fusiliers

Pioneers: 16 Royal Irish Rifles

56th (1st London) Division
Major General F.A. Dudgeon

167 Brigade
(Brig.Gen G.H.B Freeth).

168 Brigade
(Brig.Gen. G.C. Loch)

169 Brigade
(Brig.Gen. E.S. d'E.Coke)

167 Brigade	168 Brigade	169 Brigade
1/3 London	1/13 London (Kensingtons)	1/16 London (Queen's Westminsters)
1/7 Middlesex	1/12 London (The Rangers)	1/5 London (London Rifle Brigade)
1/8 Middlesex	1/14 London (London Scottish)	1/9 London (Queen Victoria's Rifles)
1/1 London	1/4 London	1/2 London

Pioneers: 1/5 Cheshires

2nd Division
Major General Pereira

5 Brigade
(Brig.Gen G.M. Bullen Smith)

6 Brigade
(Brig.Gen R.K. Walsh)

99 Brigade
(Brig.Gen R.O. Kellett)

5 Brigade	6 Brigade	99 Brigade
17 Royal Fusiliers	13 Essex	1 Royal Berks
2 Ox & Bucks L.I.	1 King's L'Pools	23 Royal Fusiliers
24 Royal Fusiliers	17 Middlesex	1 K.R.R.C.
2 H.L.I.	2 South Staffs	22 Royal Fusiliers

Pioneers: 10 D.C.L.I.

The Guards Division
Major General G.P.T.Feilding

1 Brigade	**2 Brigade**	**3 Brigade**
(Brig.Gen.C.R. Champion de Brooke)	*(Brig.Gen.Sergison Seymour)*	*(Brig.Gen.Lord HC Crespigny)*
2 Coldstream	1 Coldstream	4 Grenadier
3 Coldstream	2 Irish	1 Welsh
1 Irish	3 Grenadier	1 Grenadier
2 Grenadier	1 Scots	2 Scots

Pioneers: 4 Coldstream

59 (2nd North Midland) Division
Major General C.F. Romer

176 Brigade	**177 Brigade**	**178 Brigade**
(Brig.Gen. T.G. Cope)	*(Brig.Gen.T.W. Stansfeld)*	*(Brig.Gen. J.F. James)*
2/5 North Staffs	2/4 Lincolns	2/7 Sherwood Foresters
2/6 North Staffs	2/5 Lincolns	2/6 Sherwood Foresters
2/6 South Staffs	2/5 Leicesters	2/8 Sherwood Foresters
2/5 South Staffs	2/4 Leicesters	2/5 Sherwood Foresters

No Pioneers

47th (2nd London) Division
Major General Sir G.F. Gorringe

140 Brigade	141 Brigade	142 Brigade
(Brig.Gen. H.B.P.L. Kennedy)	(Brig.Gen. J.F. Erskine)	(Brig.Gen. V.T. Bailey)
1/6 London (Rifles)	1/17 London (Poplar & Stepney)	1/22 London (The Queen's)
1/15 London (Civil Service Rifles)	1/19 London (St Pancras)	1/23 London
1/8 London (P.O. Rifles)	1/18 London (Irish Rifles)	1/24 London (The Queen's)
1/7 London	1/20 London (Blackheath and Woolwich)	1/21 London (1st Surrey Rifles)

Pioneers: 4 Royal Welch Fusiliers

TOURS SECTION

There are six tours:
1. The Left Flank, Havrincourt – Graincourt
2. Graincourt – The Canal Du Nord – Moeuvres
3. Bourlon Wood – Bourlon Village
4. Cantaing – Fontaine, 51st Highland Division
5. Fontaine – Cantaing, 2 Guards Brigade
6. A Pilgrimage to seven large cemeteries on the edge of the battlefields where some hundreds of men from the Bourlon Battle Area lie.

TOUR 1: Havrincourt - Graincourt

This tour covers the advance of the 62nd (2nd West Riding) Division; it is best done by car or bicycle. There is some walking, but all of it is over good ground. The total distance is about six miles (rather further if you have to walk back to Havrincourt), starting at Havrincourt and finishing at Graincourt, about four miles west of Fontaine-Notre-Dame on the Route N30

From Fontaine proceed westbound on the N30 (the Bapaume road) and after a mile and a half, just beyond the British cemetery on your left, turn left for Anneux; in that village follow the signs for Graincourt-lès-Havrincourt, which is a further mile. Then follow the D15E and D15 for Havrincourt, four miles away. Stop in the centre of the village, at a complex of road crossings, and you will see on the south side the large and beautiful gates of the Chateau **(1)**. It is worth stopping to look through them at the Chateau and grounds. In the First World War it was in German hands from 1914 until November 1917; and then again from March 1918 until September of the same year. It was used by the Germans as a Headquarters; the Kaiser himself stayed there on his occasional visits to this part of the Front. By the end of 1917 it had become a ruin from incessant bombardments; and, if possible, was in an even worse state by

Havrincourt Chateau.

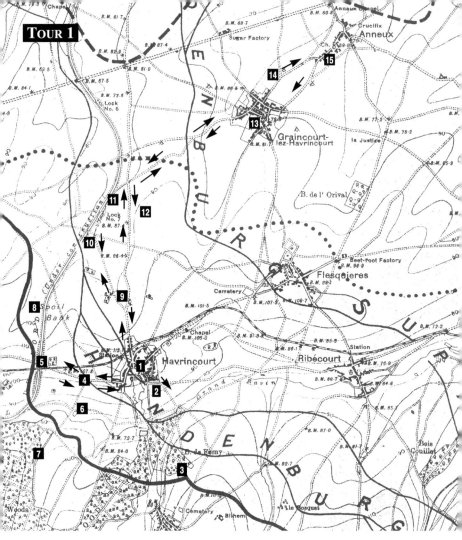

TOUR 1

B.M. 173.3 W.Chapel

Anneux Chapel
Crucifix
Anneux
Ch. B.M. 69.03

15

14

Sugar Factory

13
Graincourt-
lez-Havrincourt
la Justice

B. de l' Orival

11
12

Lock
No.7
B.M. 87

10

Beet-root Factory

Flesquières

Cemetery

9

8 Spoil Bank

5

1 Havrincourt

Ribécourt

4

2

6

Grand Ravin

Station

7

3

B. de Fémy

Bois Couillet

Woods

Cemetery
Bilhem

le Bosquet

the Armistice. Rebuilt in the inter-war years, it was occupied again by the Germans in 1940. Turn left in front of the chateau (leaving it on your right); a hundred yards or so further on there is a turning on the right, signposted to the Grand Ravine Cemetery **(3)**. After a few hundred yards you will see the tall, grey granite column **(2)** of the memorial to the 62nd (2nd West Riding) Division, enclosed by a low fence, at the roadside. The Division's battle for this part of the

112

62nd (West Yorks) Division Memorial.

Grand Ravine Cemetery.

Grand Ravine Cemetery, full of Yorkshiremen.

Hindenburg Line on the west end of Flesquières Ridge on 20 November 1917 is told fully in Flesquières in this series.

When you have viewed the Memorial go either by foot or car (usually the track is perfectly good for a car) which runs off to the right about a hundred yards ahead, signposted with a CWGC sign for Grand Ravine Cemetery, into the narrow band of trees on the edge of the wood (Femy Wood) and there, in a field at the bottom of the valley (to the right of the track – walk up the final part of the approach track to the cemetery, especially in wet weather), is the Grand Ravine Cemetery **(3)**. Femy Wood is the north eastern corner of Havrincourt Wood.

This cemetery always seems to me the most sombre and lonely of all those east of Bapaume. Here was the front edge of the massive Hindenburg Line, its barbed wire barricade 200 yards deep, filling this clearing and valley. It is the western end of the Grand Ravine, a narrow valley and a drainage ditch running along the bottom of Flesquières Ridge for three miles towards Ribécourt, a mile below Flesquières which sits high on the ridge to the north. Look away from the cemetery towards Ribécourt (to the east) and imagine that on 20 November more than 150 tanks, followed by infantry, came out of the wood along the full length of the ravine. Fifty-six of the tanks were with the 62nd Division and some of them came through where we are standing. The rest went further east with the 51st (Highland) Division, attacking Flesquières. The noise, congestion, and the thousands of men with bayonets fixed must have been a terrifying sight for the German defenders here at Havrincourt. Of the 62nd Division, Brigadier General Viscount Hampden's 185 Brigade, the West Yorks battalions, attacked to the right of the Chateau, up the slope we came down, killing many and taking 350 prisoners; but losing 150 of their own men in the battle. The tanks struggled to crush the wire amongst the tree stumps and fallen trunks.

On its left, on the Trescault road, came 187 Brigade, Brigadier General R.O'B Taylor's KOYLI battalions attacking between the road and the Canal Du Nord. By mid morning they were on the north edge of Havrincourt. At 8.30am Brigadier General R.B. Bradford VC's 186 Brigade came into the attack just to the left of this cemetery but at the outset machine gun fire from an active German strong point in the Chateau killed Lieutenant Colonel T.A.D. Best, the CO of the 2/5th Duke of Wellingtons. He could not have been many yards from where we are. We will see his grave on Tour 6 at Ruyaulcourt.

This is almost the 62nd Division's cemetery. There are only 139 men in three rows of trench graves. Row B was made in December 1917 by the Division's Burial Officer and in October and November 1918 rows A and C were made by the same man when the Division was back here in the final rush before the Armistice. The Cross of Sacrifice is on the right hand, west, side and the gate at the north-east corner. Looking back, behind the rear wall of the cemetery, there is the Grand Ravine.

Without fail these cemetery visits are always sad and this one, the first of many on the six tours, sets the scene. It is full of such very young men from West Yorkshire, the 'tribal' home of the Horsfalls; in the front row, C, grave 4 at the far end, is Private Henry Horsfall, aged 30, from Todmorden, only six miles from my family home. One might have thought that Colonel Best would lie here with the three officers killed with him, but he is not and he now lies in a cemetery five miles to the west. Many of the casualties of the day, including some of the dead, would have been taken to the rear and, when they succumbed to their wounds, would have been interred

Distant relation from Todmorden, near Burnley.

close to the Casualty Clearing Station to which they were taken. Many battalions considered it a matter of honour to bring the bodies of their officers and senior NCOs back from the battlefields for a fitting burial. There are 11 unidentified graves here, British soldiers buried in row C, but they, like Horsfall, are 1918 casualties. There are many 18 year old boys here and I always look for the youngest. Special note might be made of Private Fred Petty of the 5th KOYLI, who came from Hull: though only 19, he was the holder of the MM and was killed on 12 September 1918. He now lies in row A grave 33. The oldest man is Private George Harrison, aged 40, a married man from Mansfield, killed on 8 October 1918 whilst serving with the Machine Gun Corps; and now lying in row C grave 46. What might be thought

114

Car at the site of the German mine crater Vesuvius. It was attacked from the left. Coming up the hill, 2/5 KOYLI on 20 November. The Canal du Nord is 100 yards beyond the bridge over the autoroute.

surprising is the small number of General Braithwaite's men here, killed on 20 November - there are only thirty. Again, this was a matter of local circumstances; what might seem logical to us might not seem quite so straightforward for a burial officer at the time.

In row C, grave 7, killed on 27 September 1918 whilst serving with the 2/20th London Regiment, is Lieutenant Vivian Slaughter, aged 27. He had served in Palestine as well as on the Western Front. His parents lived in Orange, Virginia USA; his father had also been commissioned and served as a lieutenant. Every grave in every cemetery conceals an individual's story, but most will never be told. This one is not often visited, as it is so well hidden from view to visitors to the battlefields. The wood retains some remains of the German defences and needs a full day to itself – but only after permission has been sought.

Return to the village and the Chateau, to the Trescault road (turn left) and take the D5, the first turning on the right, to Hermies, opposite the long red brick Chateau wall. Go slowly and stop a hundred yards or so before you go over the autoroute at a track coming down the bank on the right and continuing (a few yards further) to the left **(4)**. This was the point known as 'Vesuvius', a massive crater blown by the Germans to give them a high vantage point on the lips and which they fortified. The 2/5th KOYLI took it at bayonet point without waiting for the tanks. Here we are on the front edge of the Hindenburg Line's barbed wire, eight rows of it with trenches in between. It crossed the road, going north for about a thousand yards before it crossed the dry Canal Du Nord. From Vesuvius, if you look south (binoculars would be useful here), the track is in exactly the same place as it was then and you are looking at Dean Copse **(6)** at the forward edge of Havrincourt Wood. You might be able to pick out Hubert Avenue **(7)**, 500 yards south of the Copse, where the British had a number of 18 pounder field batteries. Another defended mine crater, Etna, was about 400 yards on the track leading to Dean Copse, which the KOYLI also took that morning. For the best impression, leave your car and walk to the bridge **(5)**

View from the canal bridge looking north. Spoil Bank is on the left bank, above the position of the barge. The Hindenburg Line crossed over at the canal bend.

over the Canal; from it the view is magnificent. Here is the hundred feet deep cutting, dry in 1917 of course. Look north, and about a thousand yards on the left bank there is a small wood. This is Spoil Bank **(8)**, a hill made from the excavations of the canal. At 8.40am on 20 November the 10th Royal Inniskillings stormed the German held mound and captured it, the enemy fleeing north into the Hindenburg Line 800 yards further north, where it crossed the canal **(10)**.

The view to the south is of the great curve of the canal as it bends round Havrincourt Wood towards Ruyaulcourt and the two miles long tunnel which starts just to the west of it. This is part of the flat land of the German scorched earth policy as they withdrew to the Hindenburg Line in the early spring of 1917 and again in the summer of 1918. It was here the British built up the army for the Cambrai Offensive; where Brigadier General Elles brought up his tank force to go into Havrincourt Wood as quietly as he could; and where Brigadier General Tudor's guns were secretly positioned to carry out their devastating, predicted barrage. Look at the distances involved and the lack of cover from enemy observation; and think of the slow moving tanks. No wonder on many occasions they were late in arriving and the infantry advanced without them. Very little has changed on that great plain of flat land. In fact the ruined Railway Station at Ytres (south-west of Ruyaulcourt) is still there, where so many of the tanks and guns were unloaded in November 1917. You will see it on Tour 6.

Return to the Trescault road and turn left up the hill, through Havrincourt, and towards Graincourt.

In Havrincourt it was here, at the top of the street near the village green, that Lieutenant William McElroy drove through the village in his tank until it fell into a large water filled crater. A bullet hit the reserve petrol tank and the machine was quickly on fire. The crew escaped but he, firing from the doorway, killed with his revolver eight of the enemy surrounding his tank. He then put out the fire, his crew rejoined him and then, aided with a party of British infantry, he took the surrender of some 100 Germans advancing towards him. He was awarded the DSO. The infantry then proceeded to clear out the cellars and dugouts in the Chateau. There are many such stories of the 62nd Division's capture of the village.

Be careful as you prepare to leave the village, go across the square to

The village green at Havrincourt; this was the site of Second Lieutenant McElroy's battle in his tank G3. His actions that day won him the DSO.

Lowrie Cemetery from the road, looking across to Lock 7 in the middle distance.

the left, taking the D15 signposted to Sains-lès-Marquion; immediately you have crossed the autoroute there is a fork in the road. On the left is a good track going down a hill towards the canal. At the fork is Lowrie British Cemetery **(9)**, park and visit it.

The cemetery was not started until October 1918 (by the Burial officer of the 3rd Division) and it holds 251 burials. After November 1918 a further 40 men were brought in from around Havrincourt; 46 of the graves are unknown. Certainly some will be Yorkshiremen of General Braithwaite's Division. There are ten short rows, A being the furthest from the gate and the Cross of Sacrifice. In row F grave 24, five rows from the front, lies a remarkable man, CSM J.K. Rollo, DCM, MM, Medaille Militaire, of the 1st Gordons, aged 26 and killed on 26 September 1918, whilst serving with the 3rd Division. Perhaps he was one of the Old Contemptibles who fought at Mons and survived the battalion's disaster at Le Cateau in August 1914; his age, regimental number and rank all fit. There's another young Scotsman, Private Alexander MacLachlan, aged 19, in row G grave 13, killed at the same time as his CSM. He lived at 140 Prospect Street, Ridgewood, New Jersey, USA and was born in Morganton, North Carolina. No doubt he could not get to the war quickly enough, to serve with the famous regiment of his forebears. Sadly he would not see his home again and I would doubt if his parents ever saw his grave. There is another young man lying in the second row. Lieutenant Roland Bedford MC and Bar was only 20 and serving with the 9th Devons; he had already been wounded twice and was then killed on 13 September 1918. He had enlisted in July 1915 and was commissioned from the ranks.

There are many very young men here, indicative that this is a cemetery largely of 1918 casualties that holds many of the young conscripted men typical of the BEF in that year. For example, Private R.E. Weeks from Blackpool, in row D grave 6, of the 8th King's Own, was only 18 when he was killed on 27 September 1918. His sergeant lies in row J grave 9. Lance Sergeant George Strickland, a holder of the MM, was aged only 22 and killed at the same time. The oldest man here is Private W.H. Taylor from Hull, aged 41, serving with the 2/4th KOYLI, killed on 29 September, 1918. Surely he was not still serving with the battalion and had been here ten months ago in the attack on Havrincourt? He lies in row A grave 4. In row F grave 25 lies Private James Reid, serving with the 14th Argylls, and killed

117

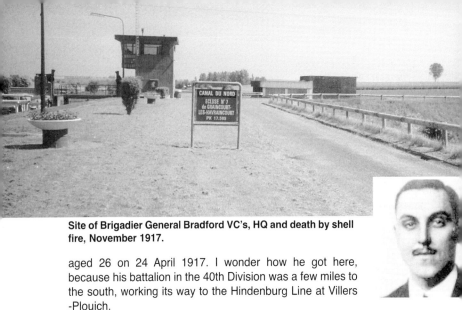

Site of Brigadier General Bradford VC's, HQ and death by shell fire, November 1917.

aged 26 on 24 April 1917. I wonder how he got here, because his battalion in the 40th Division was a few miles to the south, working its way to the Hindenburg Line at Villers-Plouich.

When you leave continue along the (good) track to **(10)**, where the Hindenburg Line crossed the dry canal. There is an old mill where the track bends to the right. It looks a bit desolate and the track surface is poor; within a half mile is Lock 7 **(11)**. Often you will see beautiful barges passing through, palatially furnished homes from various places in Europe. It is amazing what a marvellous thing the canal now is, having been so badly damaged in the war - and with the advent of the Second all work stopped on it again. Its first waterborne traffic was not until 1963. This is the place where Brigadier General R.B. Bradford VC, MC, put his 186 Brigade HQ, in the depths of the dug but dry Lock, a couple of miles or so from Graincourt. The youngest general in the British Army at only 25, he was killed here by shellfire; we will see his grave in Hermies on Tour 6. His family was remarkable. His older brother, aged 31, Lieutenant Commander G.N. Bradford, was awarded a posthumous VC at Zeebrugge in April 1918. He is buried in Blankenberghe Communal Cemetery.

Return to the D15 and turn left. After crossing the first track, within half a mile there is a special one to Sanders Keep Cemetery **(12)**. This is on the site of a German strong point defending the canal crossing in September

Sanders Keep. It stands approximately on the front line in December 1917, looking east.

Captain Cyril Hubert Frisby VC.

1918, which was stormed by the Guards on the 27th at high cost. After the battle their Burial Officer buried the British dead and 49 German soldiers. The cemetery holds 142 British soldiers of which only seven are unknown. There were two Victoria Crosses awarded near here on that day, one to Captain Frisby (who survived) and the other to Lance Corporal Thomas Norman Jackson aged 21, both from the Coldstream Guards. Jackson volunteered to go with Frisby in an heroic assault to remove German machine gunners on the right (east) side of the bridge across the canal which can still be seen from the cemetery a kilometre or so to the north west. You will find Jackson in row D grave 4, his headstone engraved with the Victoria Cross. They had charged across the 'dry ditch' into relentless machine gun fire, overcoming the enenmy and enabling their company to advance. Jackson continued to fight but was killed later in the day.

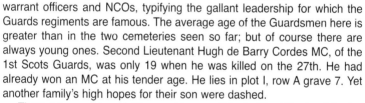

Thomas Norman Jackson VC.

116 Guardsmen lie here, nine of them holding medals for valour. Amongst them are nine officers and nineteen warrant officers and NCOs, typifying the gallant leadership for which the Guards regiments are famous. The average age of the Guardsmen here is greater than in the two cemeteries seen so far; but of course there are always young ones. Second Lieutenant Hugh de Barry Cordes MC, of the 1st Scots Guards, was only 19 when he was killed on the 27th. He had already won an MC at his tender age. He lies in plot I, row A grave 7. Yet another family's high hopes for their son were dashed.

There are a number of 40 year olds, one, Private Albert Davis of the 1st Coldstream, a married man, lying in plot II, row D grave 6. Another remarkable man, lying in plot II, row C grave 1, is Captain William Gladstone of the Coldstream Guards, who had achieved his rank by the age of 20. In plot II, row B grave 5 is an Irishman from County Kerry, Private Joseph Mansfield DCM, aged 29, of the Irish Guards.

There is a lot to think about and note before you leave here. Look east to the autoroute and then north-east to Graincourt. It was across this land that the 62nd Division came on 20 November in advance of General Harper's 51st (Highland) Division; the 51st should have taken Flesquières early in the morning and been alongside the Yorkshiremen, heading for Bourlon Wood. It would be early morning of the 21st before they got clear of Flesquières. The land here was packed with soldiers and horses during those two weeks of November and the start of December. All the divisions which fought at Bourlon were here: the Guards, the 62nd, the 59th, the

Advance to Graincourt. The 'Dukes' advance.

47th, the 40th, the 2nd and the 51st when they came back for the second time in December to relieve the 36th (Ulster). Stop and imagine the great number of tanks, some of which had become unable to move due to damage and breakdowns. There were hundreds of horses of the cavalry left nearby as the men went forward as infantry; and all the while the ground was harassed by German artillery fire from behind Bourlon Wood. Another thing to remember is that there were no natural water courses in the vicinity, only the village wells. The Royal Engineers get scant mention in battle stories but their prodigious efforts to provide water were tremendous. No battle can ever be fought and won without them. Almost exactly here, on this slightly higher ground, ran Field Marshal Sir Douglas Haig's 'Winter Line'. It came round the northern edge of Flesquières (between it and Orival Wood) and then headed north-westwards across the open land here. It crossed the 'dry ditch' roughly where the bridge on the D15E is now (and the scene of the Frisby/Jackson double VC action in 1918), and then to Boursies. This is the village along the main road, about two miles away to the west: you can see the traffic there.

On 6 December the 2nd Division withdrew to its winter line here, facing north; Lock 6, half a mile north of the D15E, was blown up, its buildings destroyed, at 5.30pm on that day. The German infantry assembled for their final assault between the main road and the D15E but were repulsed by the British artillery. Return to the D15, turn right and at the first turning, the crossroads with the famous bridge on the left, turn right for Graincourt on the D15E. You can also see Lock 6 on the left near this point. As you drive imagine the Germans massing for the attack on the 2nd Division, the Royal Fusiliers of 99 Brigade in particular, withdrawing south of this road into the trenches on the high ground in front of Sanders Keep. When you arrive in Graincourt **(13)** turn right at the first crossroads. The left turning is a minor road going to the main road, the N30. It was Kangaroo Trench, used by many as a communication and support approach. Drive to the church, a ruin then, and park at the village green.

Communal cemetery, just north of the village on the road to Anneux.

DUKES ADVANCE
20.11.17

Entrance to catacombs under the church where Brigadier General Bradford had an HQ.

Perhaps it is time to have your picnic lunch. Tour 2 is a long one and this village is worth exploring. Remember Brigadier General Bradford's 186 Brigade, the Dukes, arrived here first, the first British troops since 1914. They came with six tanks which were knocked out on the edge of the village by two German field guns; but three more tanks came, overwhelming the 77mm guns. The Dukes then swept through the village shortly after midday on the 20th to establish posts on the northern edge near the high walled cemetery **(14)**. Accompanying the Dukes were the first cavalry, two squadrons of King Edward's Horse, which were soon stopped and forced to dismount because of the barbed wire and machine guns at Anneux (15). We will explore the fight at Anneux in Tour 3.

As you eat your picnic think of the civilians here then, many half starved, coming out onto the streets to welcome their saviours. The village, like many others in the area, has a wealth of ancient tunnels and caves beneath it; Brigadier General Bradford placed his HQ under the ruins of the church. The entrance to the caverns (or catacombs) underneath the church is by a small door at the side, but it is not possible to view them. They have been surveyed and are extensive.

When you leave drive forward to the Communal Cemetery which lies at the fork in the road; once a number of British soldiers were buried here.

TOUR 2: The Canal du Nord and Moeuvres

This Tour starts at Graincourt, goes north to the battles at the Canal du Nord near Lock 5 and then west to Moeuvres and Boursies; it covers the battles of the 2nd, the 36th (Ulster) and the 56th (1st London) Divisions. The total distance to Boursies is about twelve miles. There are a number of cemeteries to visit and some optional walking.

Start at Graincourt church **(1)**. Take the road in a north-westerly direction; at the junction with the D15E turn right; after a couple of hundred

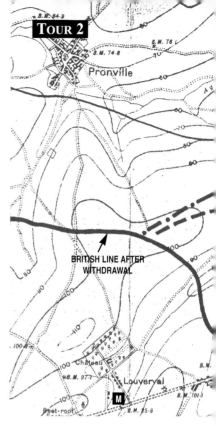

yards the D15E turns sharply right; take the sharp left on a minor but good road taking you to the N30 just over a mile away. Over on the right, a few hundred yards away is the local cemetery **(2)** and the advance position of 186 Brigade for its attack on Anneux; it will be visited during Tour 3. At the main road, N30, on the right, is where the Sugar Factory was and a large German observation balloon shed **(3)**.

Read the following before moving off from here. Well in advance of the 51st Highland Division on the right, which was still battling for Flesquières, at 1.35pm on the 20th, after capturing Graincourt, Brigadier General Bradford pushed troops forward to Anneux. They were stopped by heavy fire and barbed wire. However, he sent the 2/4th Duke of Wellingtons to the Factory and occupied it. In the dusk of the winter afternoon an unsuspecting column of 200 Germans, marching towards Cambrai, was set upon by the 'Dukes' who killed or wounded eighty men and captured an officer and two others from the column's tail. Later the 2/4th withdrew to Graincourt.

The site of the sugar factory, and a large German Observation Ballon shed.

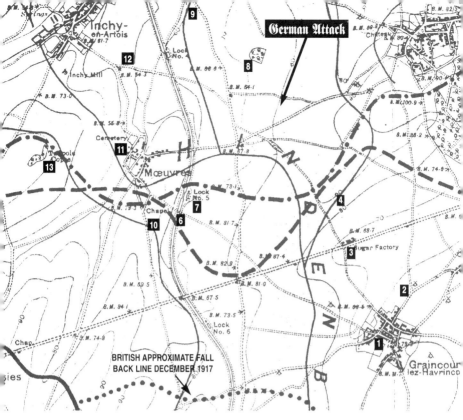

This tranquil place was the scene of 99 Brigade's (2nd Division) fight when it was told at 12.30pm on 30 November, in its positions well forward of the road, that the Germans had penetrated here to the Sugar Factory. They were attacking strongly from the open land in front of you, to the left of the modern autoroute. On the basis of this information, the 2nd Ox & Bucks and the 24th Royal Fusiliers were brought up from 5 Brigade in Hermies to counter attack; but the story was false.

It was across the land in front of you, ie looking eastwards and north-eastwards, that 121 Brigade of the 40th Division advanced on Bourlon on 23 November; they were badly hit by gunfire from Quarry Wood **(8)**. The

99 Brigade's battlefield, looking east towards Bourlon. The Germans advanced towards camera.

View from Sucrerie Cemetery towards Bourlon Wood, showing how the wood dominated the open ground to the west.

same ground is also where the British artillery and machine gun fire did such awful execution on the 30th, 'Bodies piled so deep it was not possible to see the British dead beneath them'. In September 1918 11 and 12 Canadian Brigades swept across from left to right in their assault on Bourlon. British tanks attacking Bourlon on the 21st also came through here in the first attack on the village; and this would be the gateway for all the advances to the village until the British withdrawal. Eventually, on 5 December, the 1st Royal Berks of 99 Brigade, holding on to the Factory until the last moment, were forced to withdraw into the Winter Line behind Graincourt. At last the Germans had regained the Factory. Continue across the N30 onto the metalled track going north to Sucrerie (Sugar Factory) Cemetery at **(4)** which is about half a mile away and then 200 yards along a field path to the right on the rising ground.

Sucrerie Cemetery is one long trench holding 57 graves, of which 5 are unidentified. There is one grave somewhere in the plot that cannot be found and a special memorial to it has been erected to the right of the gate. It might be thought that it would be filled with those who had fallen at Bourlon; but that would be most unlikely, as the battlefield was far too 'busy'. It was begun in October 1918 by the 63rd (Royal Naval) Division and is not often visited; it suffers the twin disadvantages of being small and some way away from the road, sitting in the middle of open land. It is easily seen from the autoroute (the A26) and the Cross of Sacrifice is usually visible from the N30.

On 27 September 1918 the 63rd (Royal Naval) Division was attacking from Moeuvres, from the west, over the canal and main road, heading for Anneux on the right flank of the Canadian Brigades. In the cemetery there are a few of the British infantry of the 63rd's left flank.

In grave 43 is Private Roland Gilbert Popkin, aged 24, serving with the 1/28th Londons (Artists Rifles); killed with him was 19 year old Rifleman Lovell from the same Battalion, now lying in grave 25, the son of Robert and Alice from Bromley, Bow, London. It is interesting to note that, although they are from the same regiment and battalion, one was given the rank private and the other rifleman on the headstones.

The oldest man commemorated is Corporal H.G. Bond, aged 38, in grave 31. The most senior man is Sergeant S.T. Shaw of the Royal Marine Light Infantry, Plymouth Division: indeed there are a high proportion of Marines buried here. He lies in grave 29.

Return to the main road and turn right towards Bapaume; after a mile or

124

so turn right at the crossroads with the D15 (Havrincourt to Marquion) and stop as soon as is practicable. This is the centre point of the 2nd Division's battles to stem the German counter stroke of 30 November; the battlefield, the land to the north of the N30. To the south is where the Division withdrew to the 'Winter Line'. It was from here that the 62nd Division, after capturing Anneux, made its attack to the north-east of Bourlon. That will be covered in Tour 3.

The 2nd Division fought here fiercely from 30 November to 6 December, in the face of very heavy attacks from the north. These came from the direction of Moeuvres and the massive German build up on the eastern side of the canal. We will go up there later, points **(8)** and **(9)**, immediately behind part of the front of the Hindenburg Line, before it turned west in front of Moeuvres.

Straight ahead on the Bapaume road, about half a mile, is the main bridge over the Canal **(5)**, destroyed by the Germans at the outset of the attack on 20 November. We will see it later but now proceed along the D15. At the first metalled track, at a minor crossroads, turn left towards Moeuvres; continue as far as the bridge, stop and park off the road. Exactly here, following the canal and only yards from it, is the site of Canal Trench **(6)**. It can still be made out, and becomes a footpath south to the main road and north to Lock 5 **(7)**. Walk along the footpath to the Lock; some 500 yards further is the minor road and bridge to Moeuvres. Between the Lock and that road was the bulk of the 'Support' part of the Hindenburg Line, crossing the Canal at right angles, to go through Moeuvres. You can still find fragments of it now, the odd blockhouse overgrown and hidden by the higher level of the fields. In the German counter stroke on 30 November, Brigadier Walsh's 6 Brigade (2nd Division) held this sector about Lock 5; from the early morning it had been under heavy attack from strong elements of the German 21st Division. On the Brigade's right was Brigadier Kellett's 99 Brigade. The Division's two brigade line closely following the track running off to the right near the Lock.

Desperate to overcome the British hold at that position, the Germans put a box barrage round the Lock and the canal crossing below it. Before that, in the early morning of the 30th, the 17th Royal

Lock 5. The scene of a German box barrage on 30 November.

Captain Stone VC's battlefield.   **Walter Napleton Stone VC.**

Fusiliers from 5 Brigade at Hermies was here, actually in the Support Line of the Hindenburg Line, just about where a short track runs eastwards from the D15, some 500 yards east of where you are at the Lock. On the line back towards the canal was Captain W.H. Stone with his Royal Fusilier Company. Sending three platoons back he stayed on, relaying telephone messages to his Battalion. Then, fighting to the last, until his rearguard was cut to pieces, he was shot through the head and killed. He was awarded the Victoria Cross posthumously; his body was never recovered.

That same night the Germans captured Lock 5 and the area round it and were not dislodged until September 1918. Two machine guns of 99 Brigade, which had done so much execution, were abandoned and lost here. Rejoin the car, drive back to the D15, and turn left, north, going for two miles, taking you through the German Lines. This will bring you, off on the right, to Quarry Wood **(8)** and the British cemetery there.

In the battle for Cambrai the Germans always held the wood. In it they had artillery and machine guns and it was from here that launched their attacks southward on the 30th. It was from this position, on 23 November, that the 13th Green Howards, the 20th Middlesex and later the 21st Middlesex, all part of 121 Brigade's (40th Division) attack over to the south over open land, were decimated by the German guns. The autoroute now crosses that area. On 23 November the guns here were largely responsible for the many casualties in the British attacks from the west into Bourlon village. The wood is quite extensive, but it is private property.

Quarry Wood is another cemetery well off the beaten track; rarely visited except for Canadian pilgrims following the men of their Corps fighting here at the end of September 1918. It is on the west side of the wood, the trees of which hide a number of disused quarries. The cemetery contains 277 graves, of which only four are unknown. It is a 1918 cemetery started by the 102nd Battalion CEF in October. Only two men here are from the UK, one is an officer in the RAF and the other a marine. A special memorial has been built to a Canadian officer who is thought to be buried amongst the unknowns. There are three plots, I in front of the Great Cross, II opposite the entrance and III on the right, the largest. All of the men here were involved in the Canadian assault on Bourlon; the 11th (Northern) British Division was on their left flank, heading towards Epinoy and the 62nd (West Yorkshire) Division was on the right flank. By and large, as in all Canadian cemeteries, the men are, on average, older than those in the British cemeteries. There is one distinguished young soldier, lying in plot III, row B grave 25, Lieutenant A.R. Kilborn of the 18th Battalion CEF, killed on 27 September 1918. He had won the DSO, MC, and the MM. He had risen from the ranks; for him to be awarded the DSO at such a low commissioned rank required a remarkable feat of bravery. It is rare to find a lieutenant (it should be noted the Canadians did not bother with the rank of second lieutenant) with three decorations. The marine is Private Mills of the 63rd (Royal Naval) Division, killed on 27 September, now lying in plot I, row A grave 30. A number of Canadian soldiers here are obviously immigrants, as their next of kin are shown as living in Britain. A significant majority of the original CEF were first generation immigrants. The airman lies in plot III, row B grave 20. Born in New Zealand, Stuart Herbert Richardson moved to London and as a second lieutenant he lost his life flying with 3 Squadron RAF. He was just 18. In plot II, row C grave 21 is another exceptional soldier, Private Swire of the 44th Battalion CEF, who had been awarded the DCM, MM and Bar before being killed on 28 September 1918.

Turn right on the D15 and we will visit another cemetery to the north, about a mile away. It is possible to see the Cross of Sacrifice from Quarry Wood. Ontario Cemetery **(9)** is on the left, at a junction with a minor road which leads south to Moeuvres. The British were not here at Cambrai 1917, and it is another place rarely visited by the British pilgrims, more frequently by Canadians. It is quite a large cemetery, with 341 graves, of which 103 were brought in after the Armistice from ten smaller graveyards, where most had died as prisoners of war. 182 men are from Britain, 144 from Canada, nine from Australia and one from New Zealand. The men who died as prisoners are easily recognised by their date of death. The whole of the area was held by the Germans until late in 1918. There is one man I would like you to visit in particular, he lies in plot IV, row A grave 9, close to the seat in the top right hand corner, the ninth grave from the top against the wall. Private Fred Kearns of Burnley Company of the 11th East Lancs (Accrington Pals), was captured at Hamelincourt, ten miles west of here, in the last days of March 1918. The Pals, still commanded by Lieutenant Colonel Rickman, their CO on 1 July 1916 at Serre, lost 240 men between 27 March 1918 and 4 April, Fred Kearns was one of the missing then. The most senior soldier lies in plot I, row D grave 2: Lieutenant Colonel C.J.T. Stewart DSO and Bar, Croix de Guerre, was aged 40 and commanded Princes Patricia's Canadian Light Infantry. There are also a number of airmen here.

The youngest casualty that you will see on almost any tour lies in plot

DIRECTION OF BRITISH ATTACK

The battlefield of the 36th (Ulster) and 2nd Divisions. Note the Moeuvres British Cemetery in the middle distance on the right of the photograph.

III, row B grave 19. Private S.H. Chickegian was 15 years old.

Return to the D15 and turn right, and drive straight down the D15 to the main N30. At the junction turn right and cross the large bridge **(5)** over the canal with Lock 6 to the left and the site of the British 'Winter Line'. At this point you are deep into the Hindenburg Line. After a couple of hundred yards turn right for Moeuvres and **stop** for a moment.

The whole of the land between the canal and this road was the battlefield of 6 Brigade of the 2nd Division on 30 November 1917; but before then it was that of the 36th (Ulster) Division. Consider the latter first. On 21 November Brigadier General Ricardo's 109 Brigade, behind a smoke screen, attacked the southern part of Moeuvres through the 1000 yard depth of the Hindenburg Line. The 10th Royal Inniskilling Fusiliers and the 14th Royal Irish Rifles made remarkable progress. However, though they got into the southern part of the village, they could not hold on due to heavy firing coming from the strong western part of the Hindenburg Line and were forced to withdraw to where a British cemetery **(10)** is now, capturing a trench there. However the Ulstermen tried again on the following day, the 22nd, 108 Brigade this time, when the 12th Royal Irish Rifles managed to penetrate to the northern edge of the village where the Communal cemetery now is. But they had to give ground when faced with strong counter attacks by the 20th and 214th Divisions, and the Ulstermen withdrew to their start line. They tried again on the 23rd with ten tanks, capturing Lock 5, but only four of the tanks rallied after the battle; the rest were knocked out. However the 15th Royal Irish Rifles and the 8th got into the village again; but that night were forced out. Try and imagine the scene on either side of this road, 2000 men, bayonets fixed, advancing through a storm of shell and machine gun fire; whilst the tanks, some on fire, tried to smash down the immensely thick wire barricades. Moeuvres would remain in German hands. Drive forward to **(10)** Moeuvres British cemetery, but before going in consider the 2nd Division's battle here on 30 November.

You are exactly in the middle of two major parts of the Hindenburg Line. Here were the 1st King's Liverpools of 6 Brigade. It was at the time of the box barrage on Lock 5 **(7)**, about 800 yards to the north-east. At 10.25am that morning, the right company of the King's threatened to be overwhelmed. Reinforcements came up, amongst them the 17th Middlesex. The battle see-sawed until the following morning. It was then

128

DIRECTION OF BRITISH ATTACK

Captain McReady-Diarmid VC of the 17th Middlesex was killed in this vicinity. His body was never recovered.

that Captain McReady-Diarmid of the 17th, a formidable bomber who had killed many of the enemy, led his men in a counter attack through a heavy barrage, driving them back 300 yards from where we are now standing. His fearlessness and disregard for danger inspired his men. An enemy bomb killed him and his body was never recovered. He was awarded a posthumous Victoria Cross. One wonders if he still lies deep underground here.

The cemetery is set off on the right hand set of the road, with access via a lawn path. There are only 103 men here, of whom thirteen are unknown. Perhaps Captain Mcready Diarmid VC is one of them. One would like to think so, but the cemetery was not started until after the Armistice, when the bodies were gathered in from various battlefield graves. By the Cross of Sacrifice are four memorials to some of the unknown. Walking along the ten short rows you will find some outstanding men, such as Second Lieutenant John Dunn MM, of the Royal Artillery, aged 21 and commissioned from the ranks after his award and now lying in row E grave 3. There are a number of 19 year olds and one of 18, Private W. Pointer of the 7th HLI from Kilmarnock, lying in row E grave 12. The oldest soldier here, aged 42, is Sergeant A.M. Reid of the 6th HLI, killed on 27 September, the husband of Mathilda, who lived at 181 Crew Street, Glasgow. He lies in row C grave 16. His age and rank suggests that he was an old soldier of the Battalion, only to die here at the last push.

Return to the car and press on to the north of Moeuvres, passing the rebuilt Church on the right. Remember we are driving through the Irishmen's battlefield. In the north-west corner, where the road leaves the village and curves towards Inchy-en-Artois, is the Communal Cemetery **(11)**. In front of it, going into the village, was the trench which the 12th Royal Irish Rifles captured but could not hold on the 22nd.

Moeuvres Cemetery is big, holding 533 graves, including the remarkable number of 262 unknown. Sometimes in the winter the whole cemetery is flooded (indeed it was still flooded in the July of 2001). The cemetery was always in German hands, except for just those few hours when it was held by the Ulstermen. Its German occupation accounts for the

129

Moeuvres Cemetery, note the flooded state of the cemetery. The photograph was taken in May.

German burials here, a surrounding stone wall indicating their plot. Moeuvres was not captured until 20 September 1918 by the 52nd (Lowland) Division after five days of bitter fighting. There are a number of special memorials to at least 31 officers and men believed to be here.

The first notable burial lies in plot V in front of, and just above, the War Stone, in row D grave 22 on the left hand side of the central path running up to the Cross of Sacrifice. Lieutenant Charles Pope VC, of the 11th Battalion AIF, was killed on 15 April 1917. Later his body was found with most of his men close to 80 enemy dead. They were defending the ground north of Boursies against a strong German attack by their 38th Division just west of Inchy, on the right flank of the Australian's battle at Bullecourt. His body was recovered. He had been shot through the head and later, after the Armistice, the bodies of the five men with him were gathered in. His Victoria Cross was a posthumous award.

Despite the hard battles of November 1917 there are very few Ulstermen here, though no doubt there are many amongst the unknown. One man who is here, somewhat surprisingly, is Lieutenant Colonel C.W. Battye DSO, commanding the 14th HLI, and originally buried at his HQ in Bourlon Village. The 43 year old Colonel lies in plot VI row C grave 25 on the right hand side, three rows down and close to the right hand wall. In Plot I, four rows in front of the War Stone, in row D grave 4, is Sergeant M.T. Harper MM of the 13th Royal Irish Rifles, killed on 23 November 1917. Next to him is Rifleman D. MacMaster, aged 20, of the same Battalion; and there is a special memorial to Second Lieutenant L.H. Martin of the Royal Irish Fusiliers, aged 20, and also killed on the 23rd.

Drive towards Inchy and after a 1000 yards or so, at a minor junction, on the right, is Triangle Cemetery **(12)**. It has only 90 graves, of which nine are unknown. It holds mostly Canadians of their 4th Division, which broke the German line here on 20 September 1918. The cemetery was made after the battle. To the right of the Cross of Sacrifice is a short row of five graves. Here is a crew of a plane from 209 Squadron RAF, shot down on 8 October 1918. Amongst those buried here are Captain D.G.A. Allan, aged 28; Second Lieutenant R.G.A. Bingham and Second Lieutenant JE

130

Gibbons. As is common around here, there is an 18 year old youth, Private TVG Nickson, a Stretcher Bearer in the 8th Canadian Field Ambulance. He lies in row A grave 7 and his friend, who died a day earlier, Private David Patton, aged 30, is in row B grave 13, the second row from the front. Lance Sergeant J.B. Adamson of the 46th (South Saskatchewan) Battalion CEF, although aged only 23, was the holder of the MM with two Bars; he lies in row C grave 8. He was a much travelled man, who was born in Peckam, London, then went to New Zealand and then came home to join a Canadian regiment and to die here. It would be doubtful if his parents in Napier ever got to see his grave.

Carry on into Inchy and take the narrow road to the left for Boursies. It is a sharp left turn at the village green and the first left off the green. Ask if in doubt. Drive slowly. You will pass a mill and some silos on the left and then a water tower. On the left, where the road curves to the left, after about a mile and a half from the village, there now remains only a single tree and some low bushes lining a hollow where Tadpole Copse **(13)** once was. This is the 56th (1st London) Division's territory; it arrived in the rear of the 36th Ulsters. Its task was to bomb along the Hindenburg Line's trenches from west of Moeuvres, crossing the valley west of the modern D34B, which comes out south-east of Moeuvres, and climb the slope to capture Tadpole Copse, then firmly in the Hindenburg Line and heavily wired. By nightfall of the 22nd, the 168 Brigade's 1/14th Londons (London Scottish) were dug in here at the road edge and along the long side of the copse, facing north-west. The Division held on here, assailed from all sides but holding on to the left flank of Sir Douglas Haig's attack at Bourlon. It is a pity there is nothing today to tell of the undoubted heroism displayed here then. The Division was forced to withdraw in face of the German Counter Stroke of 30 November. Go very slowly now and take the left fork for Boursies. Both tracks at the junction were used by the Division coming up to the copse but the right one is really only passable with four wheeled drive.

Long before Cambrai, in April 1917, 3 Australian Brigade was here, on the right flank of the fighting at Bullecourt. Lieutenant Pope crossed here going north-east, to be killed about 500 hundred yards beyond the copse. Half a mile south of the fork, where the road bends to the right, was a strongly held German trench, then the final line of A Company of the 11th Battalion AEF.

At Boursies turn right on the N30 for Louverval. Stop and look at the lovely French War Memorial on the right, half way through the village. Immediately before the Memorial to the Missing of the Battle of Cambrai

56th London Division's attack towards Tadpole Copse. Lone Tree, the only survivor of the Copse, is on the left sky line. Australians attacked in 1917 from left to top right.

French war memorial at Boursies.

Louverval Memorial to the Missing.

turn right down the narrow lane, at the bottom of the village is a large farm in the middle of a field. In its cellars a Field Ambulance sheltered in a German bunker and also in the ruins of the Chateau in the narrow, tiny, village centre. There is a good view of the battlefield at Tadpole Copse from here. It is a good spot in which to imagine the congestion, the activity and the mayhem of shellfire here then.

The magnificent Louverval Cambrai Memorial and the small cemetery below it lie alongside the N30. If possible, use the narrow road leading to the village to park alongside it, as you will want to turn left for the return journey home after your visit. Beware of the fast moving traffic! Amongst the 7,048 names carved on the panels look for the four Victoria Cross holders discussed in the book whose bodies were lost, Stone, McReady Diarmid and Johnston. Note the fine carvings portraying incidents on the battlefield – they really are very effective and show great detail. In the little cemetery look for the headstone, that of Private Clink, with a most moving, but simple, epitaph: Nettie's Chum.

After you have done all the six tours the Memorial is a good place to return to, the final seal on what one might hope will have been a real pilgrimage.

Louverval Chateau farm where the London Division's Field Ambulances sheltered in the cellars.

TOUR 3: Bourlon Wood and Bourlon Village

This is a car and walking tour and covers the attacks and battles for Bourlon, Bourlon Wood and the German counter stroke. The total distance, is about five miles but apart from the village and wood it can be done by car, stopping and viewing interesting points. Good shoes are recommended and, for walking in the wood, rubber boots if the weather has been wet.

Before you begin remember that in those late days in November and the first week of December 1917 the weather was bad: cold, wet with sleet and some snow. The conditions in Bourlon Wood were terrible, knee deep mud in many places, with an almost impenetrable undergrowth and densely growing trees. More than 10,000 men struggled in drenched and mud caked uniforms; hundreds of pack horses and mules floundering through it with them. How men survived that, even without the awfulness of battle conditions, is difficult to understand now.

Start at the church in Graincourt (1), then a ruin from shellfire. On the outskirts of the village two German 77mm field guns had

Graincourt village greeen, with a French howitzer gun carriage, next to the war memorial. The gun was captured and used by the Germans but destroyed by British artillery in November 1817.

British 18 pounder field gun near Havrincourt.

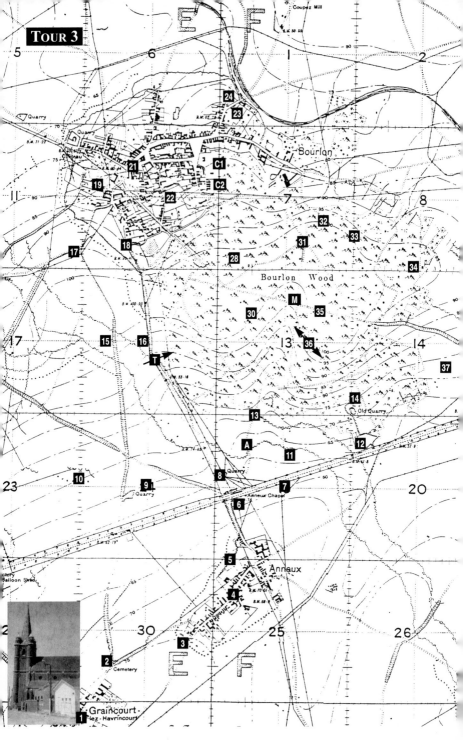

TOUR 3

5   6   E   F   Coupez Mill   1   2

Quarry

Bourlon

24
23
C1
21   C2
19
22
18
17   28
II
32
33
31
34
Bourlon Wood
M
30   35
15   16   13   36   14
T
37
14
13
13
A
11
12
8   Quarry
10   9   7
23   Quarry   Anneux Chapel   20
6
5
Anneux
4
3
30   25   26
2   Cemetery
E   F
1   Graincourt-
lez-Havrincourt

134

All attacks from Graincourt and Anneux went in here. Platoon of HLI wiped out here on the left, caught by German shell fire.

knocked out six tanks by mid-afternoon on the 20th. Three more tanks entered the village near the church and put the guns out of action; they then drove up the street on which we will leave the village, paving the way for Brigadier General Bradford's 186 Brigade. Drive out of the village northwards and take the minor road to Anneux. After half a mile there is a fork and the Communal Cemetery is on the left **(2)**. It is always interesting to visit them, as often there are one or two British troops interred there; if that is so a small green Commonwealth War Graves Commission plaque is usually fixed close to the gate. Men buried in such cemeteries are very rarely visited.

The 2/4th Duke of Wellington's held this position in the night before advancing on Anneux in the morning. Take the right fork which goes over the autoroute, the A26, and just before you enter Anneux, at the road junction, you are passing through the area of the barbed wire barricade **(3)** surrounding the village. This defence defied the Dukes and the cavalry, King Edward's Horse, who were swept by machine gun fire from the village. On the following day, the 21st, four tanks, two on each side of the road with the 2/4th Dukes, entered the village in the teeth of heavy machine gun fire from the church **(4)** and the houses. From the ferocious battle here only twenty Germans from the 52nd Reserve Regiment got away. As you leave the village turn left at the crossroads, the D15, and on the left, on the edge of the trees, was a strong German trench **(5)**. Within a couple of hundred yards you will be at the main road, the N30, and the site of Anneux Chapel **(6)**. Behind it was a small quarry, both strongly defended and surrounded with barbed wire. On the left is a calvary, which held a machine gun nest, crushed by a tank. Before going north, turn right along the N30 and drive along the bottom edge of the wood. After half a mile you will see a track running into the wood **(12)**, which is where the 19th Royal Welch Fusiliers entered it, part of 119 Brigade's (40th Division) assault to capture the wood on the 23rd. Tour Map 3 shows **(14)** the quarry where the Fusiliers regrouped after smashing their way through the first line of the German defences before advancing north. It was reported that because of the broken trees and stumps the tanks gradually fell away and remained on the rides. This is not surprising, as the tanks' steering was very primitive; all they could do was stop and then change direction by zig-zagging.

Turn around and go back to Anneux British Cemetery **(11)** and park. Before you enter look on the other side of the road towards the wood. It

135

12 SWB, 17th and 18th Welch and Lt. Col. Kennedy all entered Bourlon Wood here, the south-west corner.

was here, into the less wooded part, that the 12th South Wales Borderers entered the wood in echelon with the Royal Welch Fusiliers. The Borderers were met with heavy machine gun fire until a tank came up to help them forward. The casualties were high, amongst them Lieutenant Morgan, the Intelligence officer, who was killed by a sniper quite close to this point. Point 13 is just about where Private Plummer of the 12th, advancing alone, cleared strong points and capturing more than twenty men, to win the DCM. Later that morning the 17th Welch Regiment came into the wood alongside the Borderers and from the Reserve came the 18th Welch, led by Lieutenant Colonel Kennedy on his horse. Dismounting, he charged forward, waving his cane; only to be shot dead close to **(30)**.

This south-west corner of the wood was the main access into it **(A)**; through it the withdrawal took place on 6 December. It was the scene of the 62nd, 40th and 47th Divisions' entry into the battle for the wood. Major Stirling brought his 2nd Scots Guards across the wood from **(A)** to help 119 Brigade in the top right hand corner **(32)**, **(33)**, on map **(B)**. The Germans, knowing all this, paid particular attention to the corner and the sunken road skirting the wood with what seemed to be never ceasing shell fire. The 14th HLI, which would be decimated in Bourlon village later, came by this corner on the morning of the 24th and were hit by shelling. No.7 Platoon was almost totally destroyed, with the exception of the lieutenant and his batman. We can now visit the cemetery. It is large, in a square with the gate in the centre of the front wall. The Cross of Sacrifice and the War Stone are at opposite sides. At the back is a long row of 87 special memorials. The cemetery was started in October 1918 with 131 graves but later, after the Armistice, men were found in battlefield graves and small cemeteries were concentrated here. There is a total of 1,006 burials; however 459 are unknown and from the battles at Bourlon, Fontaine, Cantaing and elsewhere. A large portion of those unknown probably fell in or near Bourlon Wood. There are 72 men here in named graves from all those battles: Guardsmen, Welshmen, Highlanders, from all the regiments; some cavalrymen, a Tank Corps man and others from most of the regiments we have followed. I always think this is a poignant place, men who are buried here who had looked up into the fearsome, wooded hill, never to leave it. There are four main plots, I and II at the front, left and right of the gate, with III and IV behind them and the east to west central path, on the line of the War Stone to the Great Cross. The special memorials at the back should be visited. In No.3 you will find commemorated Lieutenant John Allison of the Argylls, who was commissioned from the ranks in 1915. There is another Argyll in plot II, row E, grave 9, Private D. Balfour. Lieutenant Noel Douglas Bayly, of the Irish Guards, was killed at Fontaine, aged 28, and now lies in plot II, row F, grave 7. His father had been a major in the Gordons. Near to Lieutenant Bayly in row 'D' grave 34 is Private B. Bucknell of the 17th Welch Regiment. There's a cavalryman in plot IV, row A, grave 6: Private W.C. Butcher of the Royal Scots Greys, killed when fighting in a dismounted role on 27 November and another, aged 40, in plot III, row F, grave 79: Sergeant George Carr of the 1st King Edward's Horse. He had served in South Africa. Lance Corporal Harold Chadwick, aged 18, went into the wood on the 23rd with the 19th Royal Welch Fusiliers. He now lies in plot II, row B, grave 21 and is the youngest soldier here. In plot IV, row A, grave 8 is an Australian who could have died as a prisoner of war somewhere near Cambrai, Private A.W. Croft of the 4th Infantry Battalion died on 15 April 1917, aged 34. He was probably captured near Moeuvres or perhaps his body was not found on the battlefield until after the war. Many graves have such moving stories. In plot I, row E, grave 31 is Captain C.M. Dunn, aged 23, twice Mentioned in Despatches, of the 17th Welch and killed on 24 November. A young lad of 18 is Lance Corporal J.M. Fyfe of the Gordons who died on 1 October 1918 and lies in plot III, row B, grave 18. You will find Lieutenant N.J. Gibson of the Gordons, killed at Cantaing on 21 November, in plot I, row E, grave 3. A Tank Corps man, Private B.W. Hopkinson of 'B' Battalion, killed on the 23rd lies in plot II, row F, grave 21. A special memorial, No.2, commemorates Captain David Nicol of the Argylls, killed on 25 November; he was just 20, a remarkable young man. Quite close to the gate, in plot I, row F, grave 12 is 35 years old Second Lieutenant F.G. Wheatcroft of the 13th East Surreys, a schoolmaster and one time professional footballer.

Our last thoughts should be for all the womenfolk, mothers, wives, sweethearts, daughters and sons. We visit their men but perhaps forget the years of anguish and sorrow that they would experience, their regrets and for most never having the chance of seeing where their loved one lies.

Proceed along the N30 and almost immediately turn right at the crossroads, signposted to Bourlon, and drive alongside the wood, on the D15 which, confusingly, soon becomes the D16. Almost immediately look to the left **(9)**; a few hundred metres away there is a small wood, concealing a quarry, where Lieutenant Colonel Warden's East Surreys waited for orders to advance on Bourlon. Further over to the left **(10)** was a German strong point which was crushed by the tanks on the night of the 20th when the advance of 186 Brigade was held up at Graincourt. Continue and as the road moves away from the tree line (T) the tanks entered the wood and

Looking north towards the site of the quarry (in the copse) where the East Surreys waited for orders to advance on Bourlon. The view includes part of the battlefield of 121 Brigade, 40th Division.

EAST SURREYS TOWARDS BOURLON WOOD

CANADIANS ADVANCE
SEPT 1918

WESTERN EDGE OF
BOURLON WOOD

Panorama from near the German bunkers situated at the top of Bourlon Hill on the western edge of the wood.

(15), **(16)** is where the Green Howards and Middlesex were badly hit by fire coming from Quarry Wood during 121 Brigade's advance to Bourlon. The objective was not achieved and three of the six tanks received direct hits. Seven other tanks continued, but were forced out of the village. Think also about those tank crews; so many of them were burnt to death and never identified. Do not forget the Canadian Brigades that came this way in September and October 1918 to be victorious in their assault on Bourlon. Opposite the water tower (just beyond **(16)**, in the vicinity of a modern pylon, is where the Canadian memorial at Bourlon was originally going to be sited. The view from here is not obstructed by trees and shows clearly where the Canadian Corps (with the 11th Division under its command) crossed the Canal du Nord in a very daring operation in late September 1918.

At **(18)** you are at a street on the edge of the village; it was through here that the 14th HLI and the 13th East Surreys went, keeping to the edge of the trees to avoid German machine gun fire from the village. **(17)** was a calvary (now restored) and by it there was a machine gun post that was overrun by the tanks. The minor road from there leading in to the village runs around the site of the old chateau; segments of the south wall are the only remnant of the pre-war building.

Continue on the D16 until you arrive at the village square **(21)**; now use Tour Map 3. With the church on the right, you will see that there is a fork here: the main street is to the left. The communal cemetery and site of the 14th HLI's battle at the Railway Station is along there at a street on the left. At the fork is the Mairie with the minor street on the right. The street up to the memorials and cemetery in the wood is on the right before the church.

Stop here for a moment to get your bearings. To the left is where the Chateau was **(19)**, badly damaged and afterwards reduced to an utter ruin by various people, including some Indian soldiers, tearing out wood for fuel and other uses. It was never rebuilt. In 1917 all the village population was evacuated and it was forbidden to all except those forced to work for the Germans, digging fortifications and trenches.

It was to one of the ruined houses near the Chateau that Major Johnson VC was brought, when he received his mortal wound. His body was subsequently lost. He supervised the construction of the barbed wire barricade within the wood.

Park by the church; the layout of the village has hardly changed over the decades. Consider the battle for the village, starting on the 23rd. Bourlon was always strongly held by the Germans, it was never in British hands or, at least, not until the end of September 1918. In every building there were

138

Bourlon Chateau before the war. It became a German headquarters in 1914. Below, shows the Chateau in 1918; it was thought to be beyond repair and was demolished.

machine guns with Field Artillery hidden amongst them, dominating the streets. On the 24th the 14th HLI on the right and the 12th Suffolks on the left, at the ruined Chateau, were supposed to follow twelve tanks into the village. However their distance behind the tanks was too great, and they were held up by machine gun fire from the houses. Very quickly eight tanks were knocked out. The streets were filled with Germans, who used armour piercing ammunition and satchels of bombs thrown beneath the tanks. Streets were no place for the cumbersome machines. The remaining four, also damaged, withdrew, leaving the delayed infantry, in the gloom of the afternoon, to tackle the village without support. The Suffolks did not get to where you are now. The HLI, whose task was to go to the north side of the village and capture the Railway Station and cutting, which they did; and to hold it until the cavalry came through.

The three companies at the Station (23), cut off from any support, as the East Surreys, Lieutenant Colonel Warden's men, who were near (22) could not get to them. The 14th HLI fought to the death. You can walk or drive to where it was; go along the main road and follow the sign to the cemetery on the left. At the bottom of that street, to the right of the eastern edge of the cemetery and where the industrial buildings now are, the station once stood. The area was thick with dead and wounded Scotsmen, 433 of them; only 80 became prisoners. Consider there were at least 2,500 British troops in the village then, the 13th East Surreys desperately trying to get to the HLI. The

139

German photograph of Bourlon station after the battle. Note the Germans are preparing to shift a badly demaged tank. The area around the station was the scene of 14 HLI's heroic battle. P. Gorczynski

Surreys had 300 casualties here and the Suffolks a similar number.

Walk to the Communal Cemetery **(24)**. At the far end of the cemetery you will find two French graves, side by side, 'inconnu', unknown, part of a

Memorial in the wood to the French *Maquisard* who were shot by the Germans in June 1944.

terrible story of a German atrocity in June 1944. They are two of the eleven Resistance men, the Maquisard, shot by the Germans in June 1944. There were twenty-two of them in total, including Cleophas Cattraux, whose son is the patron of the Café 'Le Tabac', in the square. That day in June the men were playing cards in a café at the top of the Rue La Sablonniere, the second street on the right past the Mairie at the right fork. A café no longer, the building, now a family home, is still there and easy to find. They were taken prisoner and put into the cellar of the Mairie. From there eleven of them were taken into the wood and shot close to the Canadian Memorial. You will see the Maquisards memorial against a large tree at the corner of the track to the cemetery. Those not shot here were taken

Victims of the June massacre.

5ᵉ et 16ᵉ Compagnie - Groupe 21A. ANNEZIN.

VICTIMES DE BOURLON 11 JUIN 1944   DÉPORTÉS DU GROUPE 21.A.

VICTIMES DE LA LIBÉRATION

VASSEUR P. VASSEUR F. CRAMMER R.   COUSSETTE H. VARET J. DUFOUR F.

CHARPENTIER M.

GAUDRON F. LEROY E.   GRÉBAUT J.   DERUELLE C.   DE RUY M. HANNEDOUCHE D.

COUVREUR R.

FUSILLÉS D'ARRAS 18 JUIN 1944   DÉPORTÉS POLITIQUE
GROUPE 21. A.

COUSSETTE A. WOITTIER F. CHARLES A. CHARLES D.   GRÉBAUT L. GRÉBAUT C. DURIEZ C. BAZOGE E.

GROSSEMY F. MARQUANT L. JAMSIN R. LEROY M.   MAYEUX L. DUHAMEL M. FRESIER A. DESCAMPS G.

The formal entrance gate to the ground of one of Bourlon's three chateaux – C2 on the map.

to Arras, where, amongst some hundreds of others, they were executed in the moat of the citadel. A simple but deeply impressive memorial is now on the site, accessed from a road by the British Arras Memorial to the Missing.

Carry on past the café to the end of this road. At the T Junction, on the far side, there is a modern house built on part of the foundations of another large Chateau **(C1)** that stood here before the war, but was never rebuilt. Turn right and then left, up a narrow road. Almost immediately you will see the remnants of the gatehouse to another Chateau **(C2)** that has also not been rebuilt, though the ground is still quite uneven as a consequence of wartime activity. This land is due to be redeveloped for housing soon. Not far from the chateaux is **(22)**, the approximate site where Lieutenant Colonel Battye DSO had his HLI HQ, and near where he was killed by machine gun fire and originally buried. He is now interred at Moeuvres. The house was close to the start of the old track leading to Fontaine.

Go up the street signposted to the Canadian Memorial – there is car parking in front of it. Take the time to visit the Canadian Memorial, with its magnificent avenue of great trees. Before the war this avenue extended all the way down the approach street to the gates of the Comtes de Francqueville's chateau. This was not rebuilt after the war; part of the site is now occupied by a farm. The memorial offers very limited views over the battlefield, but the site is beautifully maintained and is a quiet spot to reflect on what went on here all those years ago.

Return to the entrance and take the track to the left (east) and follow it until you reach Bourlon Wood Cemetery. To the immediate north of

Philippe Gorczynski with the Comte De Francqueville outside the Ferme de l'Abbaye. On the right is the entrance to the German bunker which commanded the village with a machine gun pointing towards Cambrai.

the cemetery is the Ferme de l'Abbaye, the home of the Comte de Francqueville; he still owns much of the wood. On its front, northern, wall the Germans built a massive bunker and an observation tower looking west. In 1918 the Canadians also used it and the bunker became an HQ. Here, for a time, was the site of Lieutenant Colonel Plunkett's 119 Brigade HQ.

In Bourlon Wood Cemetery, made by the Canadians in October 1918, are 226 Canadian graves, 16 from the UK; and three from the Chinese Labour Corps, who were buried in 1919; five more men were brought in later. There are only 11 unknown graves. One might have thought there would be men from 1917 but the ground remained in German hands until late 1918 and many of those killed here would have been buried in the clearance after the war in the cemeteries to the rear. As is usual for units from the 'old Dominions', the average age of soldiers here is higher than for their British counterparts.

Not unlike the cemetery in the Grand Ravine this is a sombre place, surrounded by tall trees, almost hiding it from view. The six rows running across the two plots start with A, immediately in front of the Cross of Sacrifice at the entrance, holding 40 graves.

There are a surprising number here whose next of kin were domiciled in the UK, men who had emigrated to start a new life then responded to the call to defend their homeland. One 40 year old man is Corporal W.J. Gibbs in plot II, row D, grave 6, killed with the 78th Manitoba Regiment on 29 September 1918. He had served with the 2nd Royal Scots Fusiliers in South Africa and came from Kent, leaving his wife Margaret in Winnipeg. Driver J. Hill in plot I, row F, grave 11 was killed on 7 October 1918 whilst serving with the Canadian Artillery; he left a widow, Annie, in Brockhurst, Wellington, Shropshire. Because his parents lived in Canada it is likely that he married the lady after arriving in England. There is a commissioned 'ranker' in plot II, row D, grave 11. Lieutenant Henry Metcalfe, DCM, aged 38, was the son of John and Mary of Philadelphia, County Durham, who left his wife Lily in Canada. Another, Lieutenant S.G. Moore, DCM of the Ontario Regiment, aged 25, in plot I, row A, grave 19 was a native of Moose Jaw, Saskatchewan. There are a number of men in their forties but very few younger than twenty. Amongst the half dozen of these is Private E.A. Brewer, aged 19, of the 26th (New Brunswick) Battalion, killed on 8 October and lying in plot I, row F, grave 14.

For a few minutes read the following before proceeding. The numbers in the wood **(28) (31) (32) (33) (34) (35) (37)** are locations where various Divisions and their battalions fought from. The 62nd (2nd West Yorks) was the first to attack the wood but did not get much further than Anneux. The next (and the biggest) attempt was made by the 40th Division's 119 Brigade. The Division entered the wood on the 23rd and penetrated furthest: **(31) (32) (33)**. 119 Brigade was relieved by 186 Brigade from the 62nd Division on the 25th on the right **(33)** and 187 Brigade on the left at **(28)** and on the 30th the Division was relieved by the 47th(2nd London). They would stay until the British withdrawal of 6 December.

Remember that the wood was repeatedly saturated by thousands of gas shells and men fought desperately amongst the trees and undergrowth. The wood never totally belonged to the British in 1917.

A walk in the wood (do not even think of bringing a vehicle in here!) is difficult for various reasons. The 'rides' or tracks are often deeply rutted and the ground on either side of them is impossible and dangerous. In addition, not all of these tracks are communal; most are private. Bear in mind that this is a very active hunting wood, so that extreme care must be taken in the autumn and winter months, during the shooting season; and also the breeding season in the spring. It comes as a surprise to all visitors to see how difficult the country is within the wood – treacherously swampy here, steep slopes there, rides on small embankments, giving the tanks no alternative but to stay on them. In short, do not go wandering off what look like well-established tracks. Finally, you should be warned once more that there are numerous munitions from the war still here and they can all be lethal.

The track from the cemetery curving down across the wood to the south-east corner is the old Bourlon - Fontaine road and virtually the 'front line' for much of the battle for the wood. To understand the atmosphere and the almost impossible conditions of the fighting men of both sides, walk along the track from the cemetery for two hundred yards. You will see on the map what appear to be well defined tracks. Before the war they were good, along which horse drawn carriages passed. For example, Carrefour Madame **(M)** is named after the countess who used to come out here to relax and read during the summer months. However since 1918, ruined by shells and fighting, they have never recovered. For some years after the war the stench from unfound

The Landrover is parked opposite where the body is in the contemporary photograph. The car in the distance is approximately where the wrecked tank was.

A dead British soldier by a ride leading to *Carrefour Madame*. The vehicle in the distance is a wrecked tank, which can just be made out. Note that the ride is blocked by a fallen tree. The tanks were forced to keep to the rides. P. Gorczynski

Memorial to Rifleman Oliver Bowen 227373 of the 1st Monmouthshire Regiment, but fighting with the 12th South Wales Border Regiment.

bodies was formidable, the local people reluctant to enter. Now with massive timber extraction the tracks are impossible without a four wheel drive vehicle, and even then with very great difficulty. They are deeply rutted, blocked by fallen trees, with impenetrable undergrowth on all sides, whilst the hilly and uneven ground, covered with a soft underfoot, hides many things - German and British positions and trenches, thousands of projectiles and an unknown number of men.

There are two private memorials deep in the wood, one to Lieutenant Herbert Wheelright Windeler of the 4th Grenadiers and the other to Rifleman Oliver Bowen of the Monmouthshire Regiment, killed in the 40th Division's battle. We will venture into the wood on Tour 5 to find Lieutenant Windeler's memorial.

For all the fighting in the wood the Germans were striking down from the north-east. (31) was the site of German machine gun positions and to the left, only 200 yards away, was the centre of 119 Brigade. Lieutenant Colonel Plunkett commanding the 19th RWF, was put in command of all the troops in the wood in the vicinity. (33) is where the 2nd Scots Guards came up to help 119 Brigade against a heavy attack. (34) is the location of the Irish Guards in the attack on Fontaine on the 27th and (37) is the position of the special memorial to Second Lieutenant C.F. Hartley of the Coldstreams, outside the wood and to be seen on Tour 5. (35) denotes the long track to which was the British furthest withdrawal before evacuation. Just below (36) was the double apron barbed wire fence of Major Johnston VC and (30) the approximate place where Private Clare won his Victoria Cross for his valiant duties as a stretcher bearer. Just north of (30), north of the track, is the Bowen memorial, placed there by Huw and Jill Rodge, authors in the Battleground Europe series, in memory of a relative.

When you return to the church, go in (usually closed, but you might be lucky) and see the wooden plaque which the 40th Division presented to the village; the High Altar is the Divisional memorial. Perhaps of all the battles

Interior of Bourlon Church during the war. The High Altar now is the 40th Division's memorial. A. Boyer

These photographs show two bunkers which are alongside each other on the western edge of the wood, and the view from these over the open fields.

the 40th Division fought in the war Bourlon Wood is the most emotive. After the battle, an acorn was added to its divisional sign of a cockerel.

Before you leave consider how few British graves you have seen of all the hundreds killed here and of all those badly wounded who simply disappeared, as they could not be evacuated. A great many will be found in visits to cemeteries some miles away as well as those unknowns in Anneux. Some villagers have said that the Germans simply burned vast numbers of bodies of both armies but unmarked, mass graves, is a more likely answer. Certainly a large number of the 7,000 remembered on the Louverval Memorial were lost here.

General Braithwaite's Yorkshire men were here again on the left of the Irish Guards on the 27th, with orders to clear the north-east corner but they could not achieve that.

When you leave the village go slowly back to Anneux; but a few yards outside Bourlon, at the crest of the hill, stop near the water tower and cross towards the new television pylon on the east side, close to the site at first proposed for the Canadian memorial. This was Lieutenant General A Currie's preferred location for the huge memorial that is now at Vimy. Behind it, on the right, through the barbed wire fence running along the edge of the wood, are two well preserved German machine gun bunkers, one of which you can enter and from which you can appreciate the machine gunners' deadly view of infantry approaching from the west.

The Tour is now ended.

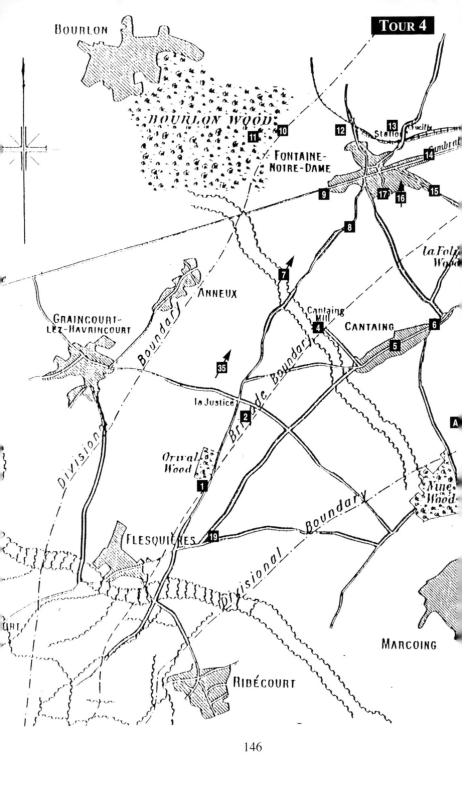

TOUR 4 Cantaing - Fontaine - 51st (Highland) Division

The attack on Cantaing and Fontaine on 21 November; its defence on the 23rd by the 51st (Highland) Division and the 59th (2nd North Midland) Division on 28 November. The Tour distance is approximately four miles by car but a good, long walk if preferred. Note that the Guards attacked Fontaine on 27 November, but this is covered in Tour 5 – which in fact covers most of the same ground fought for by the 51st (Highland) Division.

At Anneux turn left on the D15 for Flesquières. About half a mile south of Anneux go under the first part of the autoroute, the A2, then the main part and within 500 yards on the D89 turn right at La Justice (2), signposted to Marcoing. Go over another autoroute, the A26 and just beyond the wood on the right, Orival Wood, stop at the British cemetery (1). The tour starts here.

There are 284 graves, with 10 unknown. In 1930, 74 graves of men from the 51st Division buried in the Division's cemetery at Flesquières, 1,000 yards south of the village on a sunken track running to the then railway line, and 135 men from Flesquières Chateau Cemetery near the Havrincourt road were concentrated here. Both these original sites can easily be found at the southern end of the village. The 51st's Burial Officer had originally interred the 74 officers and men from the Highland Division and the Tank Corps, who had fallen in the last days of November 1917. The 135 transferred from the Chateau were men who had fallen then and a few from 1918. More about the development of this cemetery can be found in the book on Flesquières in this series.

It is not often realised that of the 242 tank men killed here at Cambrai, or who died from wounds, 163 have no known graves. Most of them were buried alongside their tank when it was knocked out or burnt to death inside it. The long cemetery is bordered by the road from Flesquières to La Justice, the D89. To the left of the gate is a memorial to the men from Flesquières Chateau Cemetery who were known to be buried there but whose remains could not be found in 1930. Plot II on the right has three long rows, with C nearest to the north wall. Plot I is on the left with four rows, though the centre rows, B and C are each split into three parts.

Here are 35 men of the Seaforths killed in the attacks on Fontaine in the first three days of the battle, 20 - 23 November. Amongst them is Captain 'Ray' Macdonald, DSO aged 24, lying in plot I, row A, grave 7. He was brought back after capturing the Windmill (4) at Cantaing and then went on to be killed almost in Fontaine. Near him in plot II, row B, grave 8 is another decorated Seaforths' officer. Captain G.E. Edwards DSO, aged 29, was killed on 20 November in the attack up the hill on Flesquières. The Gordon Highlanders are also well represented: 37 of them, killed alongside the Seaforths. They are nearly all in plot I. The most senior is Captain George Minty, aged 37, from the Regiment's 'home' in Aberdeen, lying in plot I, row A, grave 4. The most senior soldier here of the Guards Division, which helped 119 Brigade in Bourlon Wood and attacked south of Fontaine, lies in plot II, row A, grave 13: Major G.J.M. Bagot Chester of the 2nd Scots Guards, killed on 28 November. Surprisingly, this gentleman was 52 and would not be left behind at a base job. There are a number of Guardsmen here from their abortive attack on Fontaine, but Lance Sergeant James Fotheringham, DCM of the Scots Guards died of wounds on the 26th, received in Bourlon Wood. He lies in plot II, row C, grave 48.

There is an enigma in plot II, row B, grave 31, which is the burial place of Corporal A. Bielby, aged 20, killed on 26 December 1917 and serving with the 10th Lancashire Fusiliers. The Battalion was not here then, but perhaps that was his original battalion and he had been put into another as a reinforcement. In plot I, row I, grave 26 is Lieutenant E.A. Mackintosh MC, a poet who was killed at 1am on 21 November attacking the Cantaing Line along with Sergeant Ross and his platoon of Seaforths. All of the men in the old 51st Division Cemetery were involved in the Highland Division's struggle for Flesquières. Many of the casualties were caused by General Harper's reluctance to order an advance in close support of the tanks. There are three Tank Corps men. The youngest, Gunner James Murphy of 'D' Battalion, aged 19 and lying in plot I, row A, grave 1, was killed in this attack.

There are many decorated soldiers here: for example Sergeant E. Clare DCM, MM, of the 1st King's Liverpools, who was killed on 29 September 1918. He lies in plot I, row B, grave 26.

When your visit is completed, with your back to the cemetery, look north-east towards Cantaing, two miles away. You will not see the village due to the rising ground. It was from here on 21 November that the 51st Division with its accompanying tanks began its advance over the treeless open ground towards Cantaing. At **(19)**, on your right is, the road (D92) whose junction with the road you are on is at the north-east entrance to Flesquières. This junction marks the site of the Sugar Factory which was a focal point of the 59th Division's battle to stop the Germans from getting into the British Winter Line. The enemy's deepest penetration was thrown out at bayonet point near here by the 59th's men.

154 Brigade, with the 4th Gordons to your right, on either side of the D92, advanced on Cantaing, whilst to your left the 7th Argylls went towards Fontaine **(3)**, their line of attack going north-east, along the track from La Justice **(2)**. In between the 4th Seaforths advanced in support, when the barbed wire and German defences held up the Gordons. 152nd Brigade advance through La Justice, which was then a collection of farm houses.

Cantaing Cemetery at the eastern edge of the village.

Seaforths advanced on Caintang towards the left of the water tower.

Drive forward to it over the autoroute and pause at the T junction **(2)**. The 51st made two advances on Fontaine, the first on the 21st/22nd and then in its defence on the 23rd against the German counter attack. Here at La Justice companies halted whilst others advanced. In this now empty landscape there could have been 2,000 men. 152 Brigade was here and more than twenty tanks came up for the advance. Crops and the autoroute have swallowed up the old track to Fontaine at this point. What is left of it can be reached from the minor road between Anneux and Cantaing, from a slip road just north of the autoroute; however it is in a very poor condition, and difficult even in a four wheel drive vehicle.

At this point the tour will go to Cantaing first, and then walk to the Seaforths' advance. We can either use the D92, the right flank or go on the minor road from La Justice, the left flank. This latter road is relatively quiet and gives a good view over the advance, totally without cover. You will see the Cantaing water tower, your aiming point. The village was surrounded by many rows of heavy barbed wire and strongly fortified. As the Highlanders advanced their Pipers played, inspiring them into the attack despite the machine guns tearing gaps in their ranks. Ahead, British artillery plastered the village with high explosive. Surprisingly, even by 1917 standards, the CO of the Gordons, Lieutenant Colonel Rowbotham, aged 26, actually advanced on horseback. For his gallantry that day he was awarded the DSO.

The Germans commented that, 'it was a shooting match, we are shooting standing, as fast as we can'. All this action took place between this road and just east of the D92. The Division was stopped, but the tanks appeared, crushing the barbed wire and house walls. Stop at the road junction on the edge of the village, the battle map (see page 47) shows it clearly. From here you can pick out the defences, particularly the sunken road on the left. You can either drive or walk to the site of Cantaing Mill **(4)**, 500 yards away on a left bend and the remains of a right fork. 400 prisoners were taken at the mill, a difficult position, heavily wired and full of machine guns, backed up by two 77mm field guns. In effect it was a small fortress.

Looking north east towards Fontaine.

SITE OF CANTAING MILL

ATTACK LINE

At the mill's site, now just an open space with rough ground where it once stood, consider the fight against its all round defences, which were probably at a radius of fifty yards. Lieutenant Mackintosh was killed here, who is buried at Orival Wood. The fortress would not fall until the tanks came; two of them were knocked out nearby, to the north of the road between here and the village, towards Fontaine.

On the left at **(3)** & **(7)** is the line of advance of 152 Brigade, the Seaforths heading for Fontaine. If you want a very long walk or have a cycle, and wish to follow them, cross the autoroute a few hundred yards away to your left and turn right along the edge of the crop, the old track. Captain Macdonald was mortally wounded at **(8)**, 400 yards short of the village. However you can see all of this from a road.

Return and go into Cantaing. The tanks continued into the burning village, clearing it. Turn left along the main street to the church **(5)**. Behind it, a few yards south of the village, is the Communal Cemetery, always worth a visit. Two more tanks were lost here, one burnt out. Carry on towards the end of the village and take a right turn onto the D142 for Noyelles, to visit a remarkable line of German fortifications of the Hindenburg Line. After about a mile you will see them, on the right (A), opposite the Communal Cemetery, in the bank. There are others in the road lower down, but I understand it is the village authorities' intention to remove them all. That would be a pity, they do not seem to be in the way and today with banks of flowers in front look rather attractive. There is a small British Cemetery next to the communal one. Here was the northern edge of our attack from the south, the 'Right Hook' on the first day of Cambrai. Turn round and go back to Cantaing. Turn right and at the end of the village, on the left, is Cantaing British Cemetery **(6)**.

It is a small cemetery on a roadside bank, holding only 68 graves, of which five are unknown. All of the men here were killed in September/October 1918 in the advance to victory. It is not often visited, being so small, but as always holds remarkable men. There are only nine short plots, four on each side of the central path and one close to the Great

German bunkers, part of the Hindenburg Line, at Noyelles.

NOYELLES

Brigand II, knocked out on the road between Caintaing and Fontaine. This was the tank of 2/Lt A G Simpson kiled in action 23/11/18. P. Gorczynski

Cross and entrance. Captain P.J.A. Lavelle, twice Mentioned in Despatches, Croix De Guerre, aged 24 of the Royal Scots Fusiliers, was killed on 4 October 1918 and lies in row C, grave 12, the second on the right. One of his Sergeants, Daniel Mclean, also 24, killed close to him, lies in row C, grave 18. Major G.P. Spiers, Croix de Guerre, aged 25 of the HLI and killed on 1 October 1918, lies in row C, grave 1. The youngest man in the cemetery lies two graves from him. Private P.G. Wilson, aged 19, of the Artists Rifles, was killed on the same day. He came from Seven Kings, Essex.

Take the D142 to Fontaine. On the right is La Folie Wood **(18)**, always strongly held by the enemy with many machine guns aiming at this road, along the course of the St Quentin Canal which runs through it and at the south west side of Cambrai. Two tanks were knocked out, one each side of the road at the point where the high banks meet a track going off to the right only a few yards after the cemetery.

Slow down at the pumping station after you have gone under the A2 autoroute, and there is a track at right angles, on both sides of the road. Here were barbed wire, trenches and machine guns defending Fontaine; and from here Captain Macdonald was killed. All the open ground below Fontaine was swept by their fire and from La Folie Wood also.

Continue towards Fontaine. Be warned! Throughout Fontaine priority from the right is the rule, so even minor roads coming onto the N30 have priority. Proceed through this village with even more than usual caution!

The church of Fontaine may be seen on the right and to its left **(17)**, close to the church, is the house where the Seaforths put their HQ. Only

Captain MacDonald was killed along what was then a sunken lane. Lieutenant Kinnaird of the Scots Guards was also killed on this road.

FONTAINE NOTRE DAME CHURCH

The railway station (not used now) at Fontaine Notre Dame. Lt Col Unthank's personal hand to hand battle ground.

160 of the men made it to here out of the 375 who had set out from La Justice. This should come as no surprise after viewing the open and cover-free ground that they advanced over.

You should park near the church and walk about the village. Tanks cruised through here in the dusk of the 21st without difficulty, shooting at whatever they saw; but because they had been fighting all day they withdrew back to Cantaing for the night. Tank crews could barely work for five hours in the foul atmosphere inside, many men were physically sick due to the fumes and heat. The hard work manipulating the gears and steering system was exhausting and the incredible noise from the engine and guns made verbal communication impossible.

The Highlanders, the few that were there, took charge of the village. Lieutenant Colonel Unthank of the Seaforths went through the village with a few men to the railway station **(13)**. It is still there, derelict, on the north east face of the village, but for how long is uncertain. From the church cross the main road, and take the street heading north which curves to the right; follow it for a few hundred yards and you will see the old red brick building surrounded by new houses. Here Unthank and his men, a little more than a hundred of them, arranged to defend the village, knowing they were at the tip of a salient with the enemy on three sides. At **(14)**, on the eastern exit, he put No.1 Company and at **(15)**, the south eastern exit, No.4.

In your car, it is too far to walk, cross the main road again and follow the minor road **(15)** under the A2 autoroute. In a few hundred yards you will arrive at the tip of La Folie Wood and the empty, elaborate gate house. It is private property, so you should not go into the park, but have a good look at the building. There is a large bunker behind the left hand side but the walls, inside and out are interesting, covered in graffiti put there by the Germans, some in 1944. There had been ammunition dumps in the wood and along the front, northern edge, which runs down towards Cantaing, were German machine gun posts firing at the attackers of Fontaine. Return to the main road and, crossing it again to the station, you can find a number of German positions in the fields on its northern side. We will be coming here again on Tour 5. Just beyond the station where the D140 crosses the site of the old railway line **(12)** was No.3 Company of the Seaforths. The

152

The gate house on the norht side of La Folie Wood. The bunker is behind the left side of the building. The walls are covered with German gravity.

position can be seen from the Station. If you are in your car, or still walking, head west along a good street towards the water tower, at a junction of tracks east of Bourlon Wood. Tour 5 will bring you here; but where the open ground is **(10)**, north of the track entrance to the wood, was the furthest the 1/6th Seaforth's advanced on the 23rd, trying to hold the northern side of the village. The track you can see is the ancient Fontaine to Bourlon track; at **(11)** two tanks entered the Wood and stayed with 119 Brigade. Near to where the water tower is, a tank, I 41, fell into a farm pond and was trapped, and its commander, Second Lieutenant Williams, was taken prisoner. Drive back into the village and turn right. At about point **(9)** tanks came into the village, but by the evening of the 23rd the 51st Highland Division could no longer hold on and withdrew to Flesquières.

Finally, before you leave, drive to the church, park your car and walk down the street curving behind it to the Communal Cemetery **(16)**. You will find many French soldiers here and only three British, doubtless very rarely visited. Two of them are known to be Seaforths, the third's regiment is not known; all three were never identified. They lie, together against the wall, on the right, just inside the gate, a constant reminder that Scotsmen gave their lives for Fontaine.

TOUR 5 Fontaine - Cantaing - 2 Guards Brigade

The attack on Fontaine by 2 Guards Brigade on 27 November 1917 is mainly a walking tour over good ground, except in Bourlon Wood; but a car is needed to begin the tour from Cantaing and then later to visit some cemeteries to the north. The total distance, including Fontaine, is about eight miles. Good shoes are needed and rubber boots/walking boots for Bourlon Wood.

The ground covered in this tour has also been largely covered in Tour 4; for certain features the reader will be referred back.

153

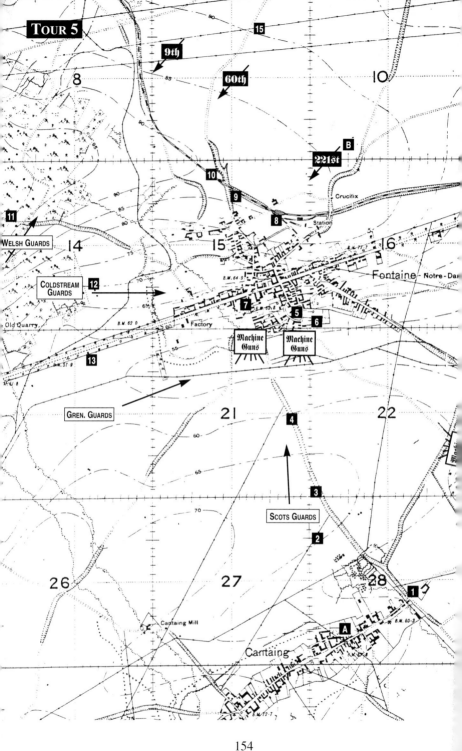

TOUR 5

9th

60th

15

8

10

221st

B

10

9

Crucifix

8

Station

11

Welsh Guards

14

15

16

Fontaine - Notre-Dame

Coldstream Guards

12

B.M. 64.9

7

5

B.M. 62.8

6

Old Quarry

B.M. 62.0

Factory

Machine Guns

Machine Guns

B.M. 57.9

13

Gren. Guards

21

60

22

4

65

3

60

Scots Guards

2

65

70

26

27

28

1

B.M. 60.3

Cantaing Mill

A

Cantaing

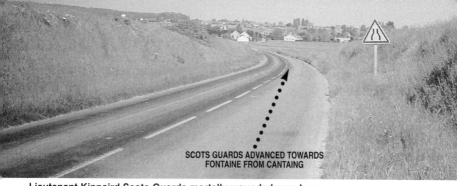

SCOTS GUARDS ADVANCED TOWARDS
FONTAINE FROM CANTAING

Lieutenant Kinnaird Scots Guards mortally wounded near here.

The Tour starts in (A) Cantaing (or, more accurately, Cantaing-sur-Escaut). On the morning of 27 November, 1st Scots Guards were in the village to provide a right flank support to the Brigade's attack from the west of Fontaine. If all went well the Scots Guards would advance north through the village to the railway line. Unfortunately it did not go well.

Go to **(1)** Cantaing Military Cemetery. Details of this cemetery may be found in Tour 4: see page 147.

Take the D142 towards Fontaine. Proceed slowly; note the relatively high banks at various points between the start of this road and the autoroute. This is the 'sunken road' **(3)** and **(4)** along which Lieutenant The Hon. Arthur Kinnaird DSO took C Company of the Scots Guards. (2) indicates the route of the Scots Guards later in the day; but they did not advance beyond the site of the autoroute.

Assuming traffic conditions are suitable, it is good to get out of your car and look round. To the right (east) is La Folie Wood **(14)**, which was infested with machine gun nests. It was thought that by keeping low the attacking infantry could avoid fire from these weapons for the first part of the advance; but just beyond the line of the autoroute they ran into heavy fire from many German positions on the southern edge of Fontaine, which brought the Guards to a halt.

Continue under the autoroute and on towards Fontaine. Lieutenant Kinnaird was mortally wounded at **(4)** about 400 yards short of the modern Pumping Station. He is buried at Ruyaulcourt. Sergeant John McAuley DCM went forward and carried his dying commander back to a dugout **(3)**, now just before the autoroute, on the south side. McAuley then took

Sergeant McAuley recovered Lieutenant Kinnaird and brought him back to a dug out. The probable site is here.

FONTAINE NOTRE DAME
BEYOND TREES

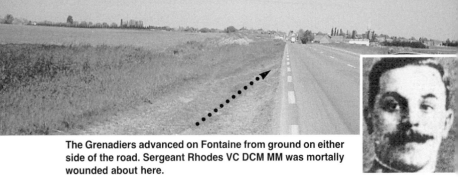

The Grenadiers advanced on Fontaine from ground on either side of the road. Sergeant Rhodes VC DCM MM was mortally wounded about here.

John Harold Rhodes VC, buried in Rocquigny Equancourt Road British Cemetery

command of the badly damaged Company until help came. His successful defence of the position, beating back the German attacks, resulted in at least fifty of the enemy being killed. For his bravery that day he was awarded the Victoria Cross.

How peaceful the scene is today; in the short battle here, in a few hours of the 27th, and some distance from the main attack, the Battalion suffered four officers and 73 men killed, wounded and missing. Drive forward; just beyond the pumping station **(4)** there are two tracks, one on each side of the road. They mark the leading edge of the German defences.

You can see the church **(5)** on the right and at **(7)**, just south of the main road, was where the Grenadiers, accompanied by eight tanks, advancing from **(13)** were brought to a halt. Two of the tanks got to the church but one was set on fire and abandoned; the other was knocked out. Another brave guardsman was killed here when attacking a machine gun that was holding his men up, Sergeant John Harold Rhodes VC, DCM and Bar, aged 26, from Stoke-on-Trent. He had won his Victoria Cross in the Ypres sector. A total of twelve tanks went into the village, but only seven came out - and these were badly holed by armour piercing ammunition poured into them in the confines of the narrow, house crowded streets.

Park at the church and explore the village. Note: all this part of the tour can be done by going from point to point in a car (except for the part where you enter Bourlon Wood itself); however, walking gives a real feel for the battlefield, and it is not hard going.

It was here, at the church, that only a sergeant and six men arrived from the Coldstream's attack, with a tank on fire near to them. The nearby

Three unknown British soldiers, two of whom are Seaforths. Fontaine Communal Cemtery.

Communal Cemetery is worth a visit (see Tour 4, page 153). The three Scotsmen buried there are the only members of the 51st (Highland) Division to be buried on their battlefield here.

Now walk back to the main road, cross it and take the street straight ahead, bearing right to the complex junction **(8)**, the site of the railway station. At the time of writing the red brick building is still there, surrounded by modern houses, but rumour has it that it will not remain for long. Lieutenant Colonel Unthank, commanding the Seaforths, was here on 22 November. On 27 November No. 3 Company of the 1st Coldstream managed to fight its way here, capturing 300 prisoners but losing, in the Company's advance of less than a mile from Bourlon Wood, three officers and a hundred men.

The Germans were in great strength north of the village and counter attacked towards it and the railway. There are a number of old German bunkers beyond the site of the railway, a particularly fine specimen in the fields at **(B)**.

It is a short walk along the street to the left, north west, from the station to **(9)**, where Captain Gillilan's No. 2 Company fought its way, also capturing many prisoners. However, they could not hold them because they did not have enough men to spare and were under strong attack. The Company had lost about the same number of men as had Captain Treloar's company.

A short walk across the field (crops allowing), or taking the road to where the line of the now vanished railway crossed the D140 to Raillencourt, brings you to **(10)**, the location of Captain Self's No. 4 Company. It had lost 40 men in its half mile advance crossing the north of the village, but had captured 50 Germans in the process. The Coldstream could go no further and later that day would be forced to withdraw completely from Fontaine. It is too far to walk to **(15)**, which will be visited by car later.

Walk back down the D140 and turn right at the first street, heading to the water tower, which you may see 300 yards away, along the curving street leading to Bourlon Wood. At the tower is the start of the old Fontaine - Bourlon village track. From here there are two memorials to see, as well as good views across to the south. One is deep in Bourlon Wood. The nearest **(12)**, in the middle of the field to your left, is about 500 yards away and close to the wood.

This is the private memorial to Second Lieutenant Charles Fletcher Hartley, aged 20, of the Coldstream Guards, attached to the Guards

2nd/Lt Hartley's memorial looking north. His is probably buried near this spot but his body could not be found after the war. Bourlon Wood lies behind.

Brigade Machine Gun Corps. He was killed almost as soon as they went into action. His body could not be found after the war, and his grieving parents placed the memorial there after his batman told his family that he was killed there. Hartley had spent his early life in the United States; he completed his education at Harrow and was due to go to Trinity College, Cambridge. The grave was regularly visited by his immediate family, but no members of his family could be traced when the WFA decided to try and restore the memorial and ensure its future care. With the assistance of WFA members and Souvenir Francais, this evocative memorial was restored; the farmer's co-operation means that there is now an authorised access from the old Fontaine-Bourlon road, although the crops have a tendency to stray onto the path. Harrow has now taken on the responsibility of maintaining the memorial.

With your back to his memorial, look at Fontaine and the Guards' attack line and battlefield. The Guards rarely failed but they did here and at a high price, losing 38 officers and 1,043 men.

Proceed into the wood, following the curving track. For about 500 yards amongst the trees the track is fairly straight but sunken and difficult because of its deeply rutted condition; on either side are banks or, when these peter out, large holes filled with undergrowth and dangerous. Tree falls sometimes block it in places; after several hundred yards, when the track bends slightly to the right, setback on the left (11) is the stone memorial to Lieutenant Herbert Wheelright Windeler, aged 20, of 4th Grenadier Guards.

Windeler had a British father and an American mother, who split their time between Massachusetts and Haselmere. Educated at Marlborough, he went to live for a year in the United States when he left school in December 1914. A year or so later he volunteered and was commissioned into the Grenadiers. He was killed by a sniper – during the same fighting which killed Hartley - and his batman buried him in a shallow grave. His body was also lost but must lie somewhere close. His parents arranged for a memorial to be erected by the Comte de Francqueville (who was to perish in the concentration camp at Dachau in 1945). The plaque was replaced by the present comte in 1983, the old one having been broken by thieves; the family continue to look after it. For many years, until the Second World War, Windeler's parents and sister came from their new home in the Bahamas to visit the spot.

Lieutenant Windeler's memorial on the left of the track. Behind is a deep German trench. The mark on the cross is where the original plaque used to be.

Behind the memorial, at the bottom of a hollow is a very deep German trench, still all too obvious. Please note that this is on private property, and you should remain on the track.

Stop here for a few minutes and consider the battle story. When the Coldstream arrived at La Justice that night after the battle of the 27th, only 180 men answered their names. Look at the battle maps. Look eastwards. Here on a line running in a south-easterly direction was 2 Guards Brigade, the Irish far to your left inside the north east corner of the Wood. The Coldstream were here in front of you and the Grenadiers to your left, down to and crossing the main road. The Welsh Guards came up behind them, inside the wood, from the main road, and crossed this track but were unable to get their to the Irish Guards because of the intensity of the German fire, who were, in fact, in the north-eastern part of the wood. To quote from the history of the Welsh Guards:

> The roads and tracks in the wood were filled with men and pack horses, shells were bursting all over the place. In the small chalet where battalions had put their Headquarters were crowds of every sort and heaps of wounded. Going forward, before we had gone fifty yards a most furious fusillade was started, the air was filled with bullets. The tracks were blocked with troops and horses and shelling was continuous, gas shells included.

The chalet it mentions was an ornate, large hunting lodge, in the centre of the wood not far from Windeler's memorial, and just short of the Carrefour Madame (see map in Tour 3) but it is now almost totally destroyed. All that remains is the bracken and nettle filled cellar, a hollow with brick walls and trenches leading into it; it is impossible to find without a guide. The intensity of the fighting is hard to fathom in the stillness of the wood today but, if there are ghosts, then surely they are here.

Return towards Fontaine. Visiting the Irish Guards is not possible, it is too far to the left and the woodland tracks are private. However if you really want a long walk, and the crops allow, then you can make your way outside and along the edge of the wood. The Irish Guards fought within it and outside as the Germans attacked from the north east. The 'Micks' lost 12 officers and 322 men up there, returning that night to La Justice with only 117 men all told. Hartley's memorial is a pleasant area to stop for a picnic if you have brought one with you. Return to your car.

Drive to **(15)** on the D140, Crest Cemetery. It is a small and almost entirely Canadian cemetery, holding 87 soldiers who fell in the capture of Bourlon Wood, village, and country beyond between 27 September and 7 October 1918. There is only one man from the UK, a gunner from the 31st Heavy Battery Royal Garrison Artillery. Gunner James Lewis, married from

Irish Guards came from left to right at the top edge of the wood.

Uckfield in Sussex, was 34 when he died on 30 September. He was probably from a 9.2" Battery. Why he was so far forward when the fighting was still going on in the area is a mystery. He lies in row B, grave 29, close to the Great Cross.

As always, each grave has a tragic story, but a particularly tragic family story is associated with Sergeant John Dick MM, aged 25, of the 43rd (Manitoba) Battalion (row C, grave 10). He was born in Gallashiels in Scotland; both his brothers also fell. How awful for his parents, Peter and Minnie in Oakburn, Manitoba. He also left a wife, Mary Ellen, in Shoal Lake.

There is a 37 year old Belgian, serving with the 52nd Battalion, in row A, grave 12, Private Paul Victor Edmund Grenade was born at Verviers in Belgium. It was near the war's end and you will find a number of decorated soldiers. It is quite likely that none of them ever saw their medal, just the ribbon. The youngest man is 18 years old, Private Chester Davies Baker, from Hamilton, in row A, grave 3, serving with the 58th Ontario. The oldest man is in row B, grave 31: Sergeant Moffat, aged 43, in the Manitobas. You will often find an American in these largely Canadian Corps cemeteries, and in row C, grave 18 is Private John Edward Kennedy, aged 33, from Springfield, Illinois, though he was born in Fort Keogh, Montana.

One of those commemorated here was a man determined to do his bit. Private G. Newton, of the Royal Canadian Regiment, lies in row B, grave 27. He enlisted in the American Legion in Halifax, but was discharged because of his poor eyesight. He re-enlisted in his stepfather's name. He was 22 and the son of Lois Ailport. There are five unknown graves here.

The cemetery stands, as one might expect from its name, on high ground and gives excellent views towards Bourlon Wood and to the north of it, ground over which the Canadian Corps advanced in the last days of September and early days of October 1918. It is one of the most important battlefields of that formidable formation; and, alas, much neglected by visitors.

If you have the time, go to Raillencourt CCE. Continue on the D140; at the T junction with the D939 turn right and the cemetery is 500 yards on the right. Be on the alert, as the road is busy and it is quite easy to drive straight past it. Raillencourt Communal Cemetery Extension is another largely Canadian cemetery of 1918, enlarged in 1923. There are 188 graves and 11 from the UK. Eight of the graves are unidentified.

The register reads like a travel book, as the places where the men came from are so broadcast across a gigantic country. There is an American who crossed the border to enlist. Sergeant Elton Knight, aged 21, of the Machine Gun Corps, killed on 29 September, came from Bradley, California and was born in Fall City, Washington. He lies in plot 1, row F, grave 1. Private Melvin Connors, aged 25, served with the New Brunswick Regiment, lying now in plot II, row B, grave 15, came from Washington but enlisted from where he was born in Spooner, Wisconsin. There is another American, who was born in Bolton, Lancashire. Private Whittle had gone with his parents to New Bedford, Massachusetts, to work in the cotton mills, as so many did from East Lancashire before the outbreak of the war. My mother's two sisters from Padiham did the same. He died whilst serving with the Quebec Regiment and lies in plot I, row C, grave 5. Close to the gate, in plot I, row A, grave 4, lies Private Waldo Lyman, aged 33, of the Royal Canadian Regiment, killed on 28 September; he was the holder of the DCM and the MM. It would be interesting to see his army record, as he must have been something of a 'lad' to have such a distinguished gallantry record and to be his age without becoming an NCO.

Return to Fontaine; but before you leave that village stop somewhere convenient, with a good view, and consider the battle here and the men who fought it in those last few days of 1917. It is estimated that more than 500 were killed in the village in the 51st and Guards Divisions and the Tank Corps. The streets were filled with their dead and the 2,000 wounded, many of whom would be incapacitated. Very few of the 16 men in the burnt out tanks are likely to have survived the infernos. The many Canadians killed on the same ground are largely buried here; this time the British were the victors and could take due care in burying them. It is estimated that at least 5,000 British and Canadian troops were killed at Bourlon, and about 20,000 wounded. It is a sobering thought on which to end this last battlefield tour.

TOUR 6: A Pilgrimage

The aim of this tour is to take you to some of the cemeteries where many of the casualties at Cambrai were buried; in some of these cemeteries, particularly the two in Cambrai, there are large numbers of men from earlier battles who died here in hospitals and in captivity. The visits have been designed so that you will work your way westwards towards Bapaume and the road to Calais.

Cambrai East (German) Cemetery
Go through the centre of the town, following the tree lined boulevard, past the railway station and when the N43 bends right you are still amongst the large buildings of the town. Be careful, you are looking for a minor road to the right, the D942 signposted to Solesmes. It is almost on the north-

The German Cemetery at Cambrai. There are Russian graves on the left.

eastern corner of Cambrai and is easily missed. Go slowly, the cemetery is just over the railway bridge, on the right, and parking is very limited alongside the surrounding stone wall. This vast cemetery is overwhelmingly German, with 10,000 burials - of whom 2,746 are unknown. You will see many graves holding more than one man. After the two wars the French wanted all those buried in other cemeteries in the region removed from their soil but did allow them to be brought here. However you will still find a good number buried alongside our men in British cemeteries and they are easily identified either by the pointed, or squared off, top of the gravestone. The cemetery is stark and magnificent. When the Bavarian commandant of the town, who buried all servicemen of whatever nationality in the most respectful way, realised he would soon lose the town in the autumn of 1918, he recorded that he handed the cemetery over to the French authorities for its safe keeping and maintenance. Sadly some of it was damaged in the fighting then and during the Second World War. There are more than 500 British graves in two areas, one close to the gate (plot VII, which contains the graves of British prisoners of war); the other six plots are within a square in the top right hand corner, holding 69 graves from the battlefield east of the town. You can easily spend an hour or two here looking at these memorials, of all nationalities. There are Guardsmen from Fontaine. Private F.H. Brown of the 1st Coldstream is commemorated on a special memorial in the top corner. Private H.G. Joy of the 3rd Grenadiers, mortally wounded at Fontaine on 27 November, lies in plot VII, row B, grave 7, close to the

British section in the German Cemetery, Rue de Solesmes.

gate. There is a prisoner close to him in plot VII, row A, grave 36, from the 10th Argylls, who died here on19 August 1917, aged 20; next to him is Private Sandform, aged 26, of the 1/2nd London Regiment (Royal Fusiliers), who died on 22 September 1917. There is a special memorial in the top corner to Private James Revell of the 1st East Lancs, who was buried by the Germans on 24 October 1916, he was probably captured during the battle of the Somme. There are more than a dozen air force men. Captain Whalley, formerly of the 4th East Lancs, was shot down here on 16 September 1918 and lies in plot VII, row B, grave 63. In plot I, row A, grave 4 is Lieutenant Leslie Young of 25 Squadron RAF, shot down on 4 October 1918, aged only 19.

In plot III, row A, grave 77 is the only American registered here, Private T. McGill, aged 20, from Delaware, who served with the Connaught Rangers. He did not make it home, despite surviving the war, as he died of 'flu' in December 1918. This was the unfortunate fate of many men who had endured so much in the war. The Spanish Influenza epidemic killed more people – almost twice as many, it has been estimated, as the Great War itself.

You will see, over on the right, many French gravestones. A helmet of the particular nationality is cast into a stone block near those graves. You will see these all have Russian names and belonged to the Russian Legion that came through England on their way to fight with the French. Notice also the graves holding more than one German soldier.

When you leave, go back into Cambrai on the south circular boulevard and then take the third major exit, the N44, the Faubourg de Paris, heading south. You should also see a sign to the Hotel Beatus. Turn left and proceed slowly, keeping on the inside lane; after a few hundred yards take a right (signposted) turn to the vast Communal Porte de Paris Cemetery. You will see its large enclosing wall a hundred yards or so in front of you. It is rarely visited.

Porte de Paris Communal Cemetery.

The men were buried here by the Germans. They used a great part of this place for burying their own dead. At one time it contained 1,521 of them, but they were removed after the war. This is a cemetery where one could easily spend an hour; sadly many of the grave stones are badly weathered and the names are difficult to see. The Register records 113 war dead, of which 93 are British soldiers with only one unknown. There are 10 Canadian, 7 Australian, 1 New Zealander, 1 South African and 6 Belgian civilians. Here are a fund of remarkable stories of men who died as prisoners, at least 26 from 1914 and a large number from 1916.

The plots are easy to find and lie below the French flag, towards the south-east corner. At the front of all the civilian graves, with no other military company and easily picked out, alongside the path close to the eastern wall and about half way along, is a New Zealander's private memorial, large, impressive, and of a reddish brown stone. Here lies Second Lieutenant

D.G. McMillan MC, aged 25, killed on 28 September 1918. He came from New Zealand with the New Zealand Artillery and had served in Samoa and on Gallipoli. He had come so close to returning to Wellington after four years of war. This burial arrangement is highly unusual – in fact I cannot recollect seeing another one like it.

Major H.C. Johnston DSO, of the Kings Royal Rifle Corps, was captured at Le Cateau in August 1914 and died as a prisoner on 1 January 1915. He was 37 and lies in plot I, row A, grave 14. A young Australian, aged 24, from Adelaide lies in plot I. row A, grave 1. He died of wounds on 29 November 1916 as a prisoner, possibly captured at Pozieres; in the same row, grave 4, is Private A.F. Paterson of the 16th HLI, aged 32, wounded and captured at Beaumont Hamel, almost certainly during the epic action at Frankfurt Trench. He died here on 29 November 1916, fifty

Second Lieutenant D.G.M. McMillan MC, aged 25 years, of the NZ artillery. His is a very rare – if not unique – Commonwealth burial plot and memorial.

miles from his fatal battle. There are a number of fliers here also. In plot II, row B, grave 22 is Second Lieutenant A.F.A. Patterson of the RFC, aged 20, who died of wounds on 25 September after he was shot down on 17 September 1916. Interestingly enough, when a book on RFC casualties was published in 1917, he is recorded as having died of his wounds at Osnabruck in Germany. Patterson had joined the army in the HAC, was wounded and invalided home in 1915 and then commissioned in the West Yorks before being attached to the RFC. He had engaged in bombing missions; and was shot down in an action which gave von Richthofen his first victory in a group led by the celebrated German ace, Boelcke. Near him, in plot II, row A, grave 28, is Sergeant P. Snowden of 45 Squadron RFC, aged 22 when he was shot down whilst flying in a Sopwith Strutter, probably over Grevillers or Driencourt, on 22 October 1916. He came from Ravensthorpe, Yorkshire.

Proceed now to Flesquières Hill Cemetery. Return to the Boulevard Circular, turn left and follow the inner ring road and the signs to Fontaine and Bapaume. Turn left at Fontaine, taking the D142 to Cantaing and then the D92 to Flesquières. The cemetery is high up on the bank, at the eastern entrance to the village, behind a large wall.

Flesquières Hill Cemetery

Six smaller cemeteries were concentrated here after the war and it now holds 914 graves or commemoration stones. It was originally made by the 2nd Division in 1918, behind the German Flesquières No.2 Cemetery, but the Germans have all been removed, most probably into Cambrai East. The cemetery was just behind the British Winter Line, established at the end of the Battle of Cambrai.

There are at least 124 men from Cambrai 1917, from both sides of the Flesquières Ridge. In plot VII, row B, grave 16, just in front of the Great Cross, is Captain Duncan Campbell MC who, on 20 November, led his squadron of the Fort Garry Horse up the hill from Masnières into the German's strong defences at the top, in front of Rumilly. He was killed after only a few yards of that heroic but suicidal charge. The largest number here, from any formation, are the 52 New Zealanders from their battle to cross the St Quentin Canal at Crèvecoeur in September 1918, the same battleground of the 'Right Hook' at Cambrai in November 1917. There are a number of airforce men. One lies in plot IV, row B, grave 21. Lieutenant Charles F. Drabble, aged 21, of 18 Squadron RFC, was killed on 13 August 1918; he was flying a DH4; the other member of his crew, Second Lieutenant RW Rawley, is also buried here.

There are ten Tank Corps men buried here. Prominent amongst them in plot III, row B, grave 6 is Lance Corporal G.C. Foot DCM, aged only 20,

Flesquières Hill Cemetery. There are extensive views to the north. In the middle distance, to the right of the Cross of Sacrifice, is Orival Wood.

killed in the attack on Flesquières. Another is in plot VIII, row E, grave 10. Second Lieutenant R.A. Jones of D Battalion, commanding the female tank D41, was also killed on the 20th. Near him, in row D, grave 5, is Gunner Trevor Lawley, aged 37 from G Battalion, another 20 November casualty. He came from Ross-on-Wye. The most senior officer here is Lieutenant Colonel R.S. Walker DSO, a sapper who was killed on 30 September 1918, at 46 the oldest man in the cemetery register. He is buried in plot I, row D, grave 1, near the pavilion. Farrier Sergeant T. Wiseman (plot VIII, row I, grave 2), held the Long Service and Good Conduct Medal. He joined the 18th Hussars when he was 15 years old, and was killed here on 21 November 1917, aged 33.

Before leaving the high ground of the cemetery, note the excellent view that the British had from their Winter Line. Drive slowly into the village and stop at the village green, just beyond the crossroads. On the right you will see two memorials, one to a tragic incident in 1940 in which a number of French soldiers were killed by the Germans. The other is in memory of Corporal Johannes Bergmann, aged 27, commanding a troop of the U.S. 113 Reconnaissance Squadron, and the first man to enter the village in its liberation on the 2nd of September 1944. Many photographs were taken of him and his few men, with his jeep surrounded by the delighted villagers. Later that day, as he led his small column on the road to Cantaing, he was killed by a sniper. The villagers took him to their cemetery and, with all ceremony, buried him there, the whole population following his coffin. In 1948 he was taken home and reinterred at Oak Hill, Parkerburg, Iowa. Each year on the anniversary of their liberation he is remembered.

There is now a Mk IV tank, 'Deborah', dug out of the ground on the edge of the village in November 1998 by Philippe Gorczynski. It is now in a barn close to the green, the doors of which are decorated by British and French flags. It will eventually become part of a bigger memorial project planned for the village. It is believed that there are at least two other tanks lying somewhere in the nearby fields.

The tour is now heading for the two British cemeteries at Hermies. Drive out of the village on the ridge top road to Havrincourt. At a suitable moment look at the marvellous views to the south. This is the area of the so-called 'Flanders Sanatorium'. Coming towards you on 20 November were hundreds of tanks and thousands of infantry men battling their way through the Hindenburg Line. Coming towards you up the hill was the 51st (Highland) Division and on the right the 62nd (West Riding). Drive through Havrincourt and take the D5 to Hermies over the great cutting of the Canal Du Nord. Take the right hand road, still on the D5 towards Doignies and then at the western edge of the village take the D19 signposted to Bertincourt. Both cemeteries are close to the village on its western side, one on the right hand side of the road and the much larger one immediately opposite.

Hermies British Cemetery

Hermies British Cemetery is the small one, behind British lines after the

3rd Australian Infantry Battalion captured it on 9 April 1917, until it was lost on 22 March 1918, not to be recaptured until the following September. The register records 108 graves, of which 3 are unknown. The best known burial in this cemetery is Brigadier General 'Boys' Bradford VC. He was killed at Lock 7 (see Tour 1) at the age of 25. He had won his Victoria Cross in front of the Butte de Warlencourt twelve months earlier, in the last stages of the 1916 Battle of the Somme. Close to him is the first chaplain seen thus far, though there are many buried amongst their men all over the Western Front. Reverend George Harvey Ranking, from Haselmere, in Surrey, was aged 46 when he was mortally wounded on 20 November 1917. Private H.V. Christmas, aged 19, came from Shoreham-on-Sea, but was serving with the 2nd Battalion Australian Infantry when he was killed on 22 April 1917. He lies in row C, grave 4. In row F, grave 12 is Second Lieutenant A.R. Chapman, aged 26, who had enlisted in the Royal Fusiliers in 1914 and was commissioned in September 1916 into the Machine Gun Corps. He was killed at Moeuvres on 2 December 1917.

Walk across the road, up the long approach to

Hermies Hill Cemetery.

This is a large cemetery with 1,005 graves, 297 of then unidentified. The men buried and commemorated here indicate the intensely fought battles in the area - of the German attacks and withdrawal in 1918 and of course Cambrai in 1917 and the advance to victory in 1918. The village of Hermies was adopted by the Yorkshire industrial town of Huddersfield after the war – appropriately, because so many of the 62nd Division lie here. It is likely that a fair number of them lie in the unknown graves. Four other cemeteries were incorporated to this one, 136 men reinterred after the Armistice.

At the entrance on the right is the War Stone and in front of it, in plot III, row B, grave 5, is Second Lieutenant Frank Edward Young VC, aged 23, killed on 18 September 1918 whilst serving with the 1st Herts. He was last seen fighting hand to hand – severe fighting that lasted four hours – south-east of Havrincourt after performing

Frank Edward Young VC.

Hermies Hill.

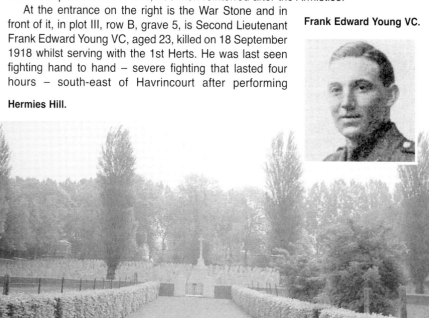

incredible feats of courage during an enemy counter attack under an intensive German bombardment. Amongst other things he rescued two men from capture and although surrounded fought his way back to the main barricade. There are 235 men here who were brought back from the battlefields we have been viewing, either killed or dying from wounds. One young 21 years old Welshman from Pwllehli had gone into Bourlon Wood with the 19th Royal Welch Fusiliers. He now lies in plot I, row C, grave 15, close to the War Stone. CSM H.C. Wing MM and Bar, of the 13th Royal Fusiliers, killed on 4 September 1918, lies in plot IV, row C, grave 10. In plot I, row F, grave 37, is a highly decorated American who served with the King's Liverpools and was killed on 30 December 1917. Frank Mossop, a sergeant, was barely 21 and already the holder of the DCM and Bar and the MM. His family lived in Sewickly, Pennsylvania.

A doctor is remembered by Special Memorial No.1, in the top left hand corner. Captain J.M. Matheson from Edinburgh was 27 when he was killed on 3 November 1917. CSM E. Irving DCM and Bar, a Coldstreamer (IV G 3), died on 27 September 1918. CQMS John Harvey (I G 24), aged 25 of the 10th Lancashire Fusiliers, died on 25 February 1918 just before the great German Spring attack. He had enlisted in August 1914. There is a Marine in plot 'IV' row 'J' grave 1, Captain F.G.Elliot MC, Croix de Guerre, aged 28 and killed on the 27th of September 1918. There are so many we would like to visit but here in plot 'I' row 'H' grave 23 is Captain Henry Lancaster Neville Dundas MC and Bar (I, H, 23), of the 1st Scots Guards aged 21 and killed on 27 September 1918. He had served as the Battalion's adjutant and bombing officer, and also Brigade bombing officer; he was killed in the crossing of the Canal du Nord; he was present at the Battalion's action on 27 November 1917.

Private H. Care from Lincoln (IV D 29) was an 18 year old of the Devonshires, killed on 18 September 1918. Another young hero, aged 19, is Lieutenant T.M. Bennet MC of the RFC (I A 5) who was shot down on 10 November 1916. He was shot down over Havrincourt Wood at 11.30 am whilst flying in a Sopwith Strutter by Leutnant von Keudell; the body of his fellow crew member, Second Lieutenant Allport, was never found, and he is commemorated on the Air Force Memorial at Arras.

Continue on the D19 southwards towards Bertincourt and then turn left at the second bridge over the Canal du Nord, the D19E to Ruyaulcourt. Go slowly over the canal and where the road bends at the village, stop. The British Cemetery lies 400 yards to the left down a narrow sunken track, once the site of many field batteries. You should park and walk unless you want a long reverse back; in addition the track is frequently used by tractors towing farm equipment and you would block it; as it is sunken there is no way out.

Ruyaulcourt Military Cemetery

The 42nd (East Lancashire) Division was in the area in the spring of 1917, chasing the Germans back to the Hindenburg Line and a great many of its men are still here, rows of Lancashire Fusiliers, East Lancs and

Ruyaulcourt Military Cemetery.

Manchesters; and gunners killed by counter bombardments. Lieutenant the Hon. A.M.Kinnaird MC (F 15), aged 32, of the 1st Scots Guards, was mortally wounded on 27th November 1917 before Fontaine and rescued by Sergeant McAuley VC, DCM (see Tour 5). Lieutenant Colonel Best DSO and Bar, aged 28, was killed whilst commanding the 2/5th Dukes at Havrincourt Chateau on 20 November (see Tour 1). He now lies close to Lieutenant Kinnaird. Once again the cemetery is full of sad but wonderful stories.

There are men from my father's B/210 Burnley Battery RFA and Private W.R.Daniels aged 23 of the East Lancs Field Amnbulance is lying next to Lieutenant Kinnaird. Private A. F. Nicholson (N 30), one of my father's friends, died as a prisoner on 21 September 1916. Corporal Richard Robinson (E 10) of the Burnley Battery was killed on 13 July 1917. Captain G. Walker MC (F 13), aged 27, of the RAMC, was killed in Bourlon Wood on 27 November 1917.

Before you leave look across the sunken road towards the battlefields of 1917 and 1918.

Drive into Ruyaulcourt and remain on the D19E to Ytres. Turn left and go over the A2 autoroute. Drive slowly into the village

The entrance to a two mile long stretch of tunnel for the Canal du Nord. It runs between Ytres (photograph) and Ruyaulcourt.

The railway station at Ytres photographed in 1999 (above) and in 1918 (right). It was the site of tank unloading for the Battle of Cambrai.

Tank trains awaiting dispatch to forward detraining railheads, 20 November 1917.

and at the road junction go straight across, down a street on the east side of the village until you arrive at a crossroads. Turn left and you will see a water tower on the right at a fork. Stop there. If you walk a hundred yards straight ahead you will come to the Canal du Nord and the start of the two mile long tunnel to Ruyaulcourt.

Rejoin your car, go left at the first cross roads and, at the next turn, left on the D18. You will skirt a small wood will see the old railway station where many of the tanks for Cambrai were unloaded. Drive up the hill, now the D43, and the large cemetery is on the right at the ridge top. Turn right on the main road, the D172 and park near the entrance of

Rocquigny – Equancourt Road British Cemetery.

Look south-east, down the road to the canal bridge, where you will see the workings of a large quarry; in 1944 there was a rocket fuel plant there.

The cemetery is very big, holding almost 2,000 graves. It was begun in 1917 and holds many of the casualties from Bourlon and Fontaine. There are only 22 unnamed graves; until the British withdrawal in March 1918 it was used by the 21st and 48th Casualty Clearing Stations. The field across the road was a gigantic encampment of their tents and temporary buildings, as was the slope behind the cemetery. Many of the men were buried by the Germans after March 1918, who called it Etricourt Old British Cemetery. Stand at the entrance and look at its vastness; knowing it was the cemetery for the CCS, consider that most of the men were wounded, brought here from the battlefields. The work of stretcher bearers and field ambulances in unimaginably awful conditions was tremendous. There must have been a quarter of a million men in the land about here and tens of thousands of horses and mules. Think also of the awful confusion on 21 March 1918 as the Germans hammered their way through here to the west. How did they manage to get wounded and staff away? How many had to be abandoned and left as prisoners? In my count of those here I estimate that there are at least 750 from the Bourlon/Cambrai battles and all of the regiments we have talked about are represented: Guards, Londonders, Welshmen, Midlanders, Irishmen, Scotsmen, Yorkshiremen and Lancastrians, many from the North-East and the southern counties. There are men of the infantry, cavalry, tank corps, gunners, RAF, RFC, Germans, French civilians and even an Italian

Rocquigny-Equancourt Road Cemetery.

171

– a truly representative gathering of the military efforts in this area.

Under a tree close to the wall alongside the road (III E) is Sergeant J.H.Rhodes VC, DCM and Bar, mortally wounded at Fontaine when the Grenadiers assaulted the village from the west (see Tour 5). Very close to him in III E are two soldiers who died with the 12th South Wales Borderers in Bourlon Wood. Grave 26 holds Captain J.E. Jenkins and next to him is Corporal T.G.James DCM, 21, from Cardiff. One of their comrades, a 19 year old, Private J. Freeman (V A 9) who died of wounds, lies only yards from his captain. Near to the Great Cross of Sacrifice is a 54 years old man, Private A.J. Batchelor (X D 9) of the 724th Labour Company, who died of wounds on 19 February 1918, just before the German attack. He is the oldest man in the register here; he came from Kilburn, leaving behind Louise his wife.

Second Lieutenant F.G. Budd (XIII D 37) MC MM, commissioned from the ranks into the 16th KRRC, died aged 27 on 15 October 1918. A 19 year old American from Hawthorne, California, Lieutenant W.M. Clark (II C 14), who served with the 1/7th Black Watch, died on 20 November 1917. Lieutenant E.W. Horner (I E 23) 18th Hussars, aged 28, enlisted with the North Staffs Yeomanry in 1914 and transferred to the Hussars in 1915; he was seriously wounded, but rejoined in 1916. He was mortally wounded, dying of his wounds on 21 November.

There is a remarkable man in plot VI, row B, grave 11: Private The Lord Edward Beauchamp Seymour aged 38, the son of the Marquess of Hereford, served with Lord Strathcona's Horse, dying of wounds on 5 December 1917. What a story there must be here.

This is an ideal spot to have a picnic and to contemplate this 'Silent City' and the sacrifices of so many men in the fighting of 1917 and 1918.

The 'Pilgrimage Tour' is now complete. You have travelled through some historic British military country, still 'occupied' by thousands of our men. As a last word, the Military cemetery at Bancourt, 400 yards right of the road, the D7 to Haplincourt, holds Victoria Cross hero Sergeant Jones and the small Communal Cemetery opposite holds a few of our RFC and RAF flyers.

172

INDEX